WOODLAND WALKS
in Scotland

WOODLAND WALKS
in Scotland
Gerald Wilkinson

First published in Great Britain in 1986 by
Webb & Bower (Publishers) Limited,
9 Colleton Crescent, Exeter, Devon EX2 4BY, and
Ordnance Survey,
Romsey Road, Maybush, Southampton S09 4 DH
in association with
Michael Joseph Limited,
27 Wright's Lane, London W8 5SL

Designed by Peter Wrigley

Production by Nick Facer

British Library Cataloguing in Publication Data

Wilkinson, Gerald
    The Ordnance Survey woodland walks in Scotland.
    1. Forests and forestry — Scotland
    2. Scotland — Description and travel — 1981-
    — Guide-books
    I. Title
    914.11'04858   DA870
    ISBN 0–86350–062–5

Typeset in Great Britain by Keyspools Limited, Golborne, Lancashire
Printed and bound in Great Britain by Hazell Watson and Viney Limited,
Member of the BPCC Group, Aylesbury, Bucks

TITLE PAGE
The shores of Loch Eil are typically clothed in oak and birch,
but a promontory dramatically displays the native pine

Contents

Introduction

Take the high road, and you will see many Scottish forests; but these are not the true Scottish woodlands. Looking for woods of oak, ash, alder, even birch (though there are birches everywhere) takes you on a sort of low road into a more intimate Scottish countryside a little removed from the traditional scenery of open muirs and grand mountains. The oakwoods which once filled all the valleys are nearly all gone – mostly they are nature reserves and they are identified in this book. Also protected and defined are the surviving remnants of the original Caledonian pine forest which once clothed all the hills up to 2000 feet. To find all the woods there are long distances to travel but the distances are made smooth by good roads and they are full of air and space, and, in the Highlands, of a heady beauty that is peculiarly Scotland's.

SOUTH

The high road to Galloway is no fun, and you might turn north-west at Dumfries to peaceful Moniaive and a look at the juniper wood of Tynron. This is unique and it is a revelation. Then your route to the Galloway Forest Park and associated woody places will be untroubled by diesel fumes. The Wood of Cree, a perfect oakwood now largely in the hands of the RSPB, is another point of pilgrimage – not unique but rare enough. I suppose the time will come when it has to be fenced and people queue to see it. Other good things come from the Cree and there is plenty to occupy anyone in Galloway for a fortnight or so, including a fascinating coastline.

For the Border country you can desert the high road (A7) soon after Carlisle, turning onto the B6357 at Canonbie, a plain but spacious town where it is wise to fill the petrol tank. There are no ancient woodlands, only vast new forests, on this route, and Kielder village is not even in Scotland, but I think you will find the views inspiring. Arriving at Bonchester Bridge you can get through Hawick easily by heading back to Carlisle for a mile or two, then right to Robertown and the attractive 'no through road' to Craik, the centre of a new forest in a rich old countryside.

From here the way north is easy and delightful to the Tweed and another revelation at Dawyck. This very fine arboretum is now in the care of Edinburgh Royal Botanic Gardens. From Edinburgh it is to be reached smoothly by the A701.

North of the Tweed and bordered by sea the country may be seen as peculiarly Edinburgh's, and not much frequented by English holiday-makers. No one would travel far to see Vogrie Country Park or Pressmennan Wood, but these and Dunbar, with its wide Country Park, surrounding elmy countryside and the backing of the Lammermuir hills, are worth thinking about.

WEST

Unless you find a devious route to the Gourock Ferry (and it is hard driving whichever way you go) you will not reach the western Highlands without some experience of the high road. The old song leads us to Loch Lomond whose bonnier banks, with alder, birch and oakwood, are reached by a decidedly low road on the east side.

Five miles of water from Gourock (or seventy-five of road from Glasgow) bring you to Dunoon, thence to a forested mountain country which must closely resemble the original. The Benmore Forest was planted, but a long time ago and on a large scale. The trees are often Norway spruce, not a native tree since it failed to recover ground after the Ice – but the trees do look indigenous. Two major tree collections are here, and two more not far away on Loch Fyne, at Inveraray and Crarae.

From Inveraray in the direction of Oban could be your route to several oakwoods of the western Highlands. The road is smooth, and uncluttered except by too frequent concrete litter bins in lay-bys where you may not sleep – but it is the high road, after all. Most of the Caledonian pinewood relics are in the central

Highlands, one of the most famous being the Black Wood of Rannoch. It is Rannoch Muir that you cross on the way from Loch Lomond to Glencoe. The moor is a forbidding tract apparently in the state it was left by the prehistoric ice (while Glencoe manages to look historic as well as awe-inspiring). To get to the pinewood of Rannoch by car you must take an eastern route, but it may be worth mentioning that you can travel by train to Rannoch Station for the only western approach. A western route northwards by car offers you the temptation of a heroic detour to Morvern, and I believe you would not regret it. You might even have time for Mull, which I didn't.

North of Fort William you are stuck with the high road because there is no other. But it is a fine experience, whatever the weather, and the road gradually shrinks until north of Loch Alsh it is little wider than a Surrey lane. Even if you are only here for the woodlands, Skye beckons romantically. And Skye has something to say about trees in a larger context of sea and rock. From Kyle of Lochalsh you have an alternative coast road to Loch Carron, thence to Kishorn for another of those Scottish revelations, Rassal Ashwood. It is so small in the great desert nibbled by the sheep, and yet so unbelievably fecund.

Northward lie Torridon and Maree, arguably Scotland's most beautiful places, with the first of Britain's nature reserves enclosing some native pines, and with inspiring mountains at least equal to Skye's. Inverewe Gardens, with sub-tropical palms, is just beyond Loch Maree and is probably the end of the road for many tourists – it is certainly a climax. But there are large and serious nature reserves further north, with woodlands. There is also an impressive walk that is not mentioned in the text: Corrie Shallock Gorge, heavily wooded and belonging to the National Trust for Scotland (as does Inverewe).

Loch Maree can be approached from the east – from Inverness. By Inverness also is the route south-westwards, along the shore of Loch Ness as far as Drumnadrochit, to Glen Affric, for its important native pinewood, and a long walk in the very heart of the Highlands. The road northwards from Inverness will take

you to the Shin Forest – one walk here is in surprising richness of vegetation – and you could strike out westwards here for Glen Einig, another home of the native pine. From Lairg to the northern forests of Naver and Borgie the road is long, but you will find absolute peace.

EAST

From Edinburgh, or at least from Queensferry, the high road sweeps grandly northwards, so smoothly that you might miss the undoubted charms of the Lomond Hills, Ladybank and Tentsmuir, and arriving unexpectedly soon at Perth, might be swept on past Kinnoull and the Kinfauns Forest. My route would take you quietly by Scone Palace, Glamis Castle and to the ultimate quietness of Montreathmont Forest. But only the silence, and a few wild flowers, are indigenous – unless the birches of Kinnoull have long pedigrees.

You could continue north from Montreathmont, into Aberdeen or the Middle Dee, but the high road to the north is the A9. It is a well-established route, for the Romans knew it well as far as Inchtuthill, just north of Perth. This most northerly Roman fort is not a woodland site, except that it was made of wood and it would be extremely interesting to know what species of tree they felled for its 12-inch-square posts. Archaeologists have them of oak, which the soldiers brought from England. This is ridiculous of course – there must have been plenty of oak. Beech also grew by the Tay in prehistoric times. Anyway, what would have been wrong with pine, not so lasting but abundantly easy to replace? Even more ridiculous is the picture of the decamping Romans rooting up their massive posts and solemnly bearing them southwards through the forest, but that is the theory. Even then they left all their nails, 12 tons of them (perhaps this was a misprint for ½ ton).

Dunkeld, not much further north, is a great centre for trees and walkers. The Dunkeld larch combines the best qualities of the European and the Japanese larches, and the name of Atholl is a very honourable one in the history of British forestry. Between Dunkeld and Blair Atholl is a string of nature reserves amongst woodland of broadleaves planted by

the Dukes. But Pitlochry and the Pass of
Killiecrankie have too much of the high road
about them for my liking. Turn left at Linn of
Tummel for the low road to Rannoch's Black
Wood, or continue through Glen Garry for
Kingussie and Aviemore.

The best known and the largest native
pinewood is at Rothiemurchus in the
Cairngorm National Nature Reserve, Britain's
largest reserve of nearly 59,000 acres. There is
a complex of nature reserves here including a
native birchwood at Craigielachie, not far from
the high road, A9. The Glen More Forest Park
is also part of the complex. There are superb
views here of thousands of acres of mixed pine
and birch, and you can see capercaillies, which
are large enough even for me to see. I read that
you might also see golden eagles, ptarmigan,
dotterel, greenshank and snow bunting.

The ancient forest of Mar is on the south-
east side of the Cairngorm NNR, and can be
reached by a long walk, but the road to
Braemar is the A93 from Perth. From the Linn
of Dee, near Braemar, to Crathes Castle, 15
miles from Aberdeen, is a belt of really fine and
accessible country, with some woodland sites
of great interest. You could do worse than aim
for Middle Deeside to the exclusion of
everywhere else.

Above Aberdeen is a vast triangle of fairly
low country, a land of castles, great houses and
gardens, remote to Sassenachs but perfectly
sophisticated, with factory farming and finnan
haddocks, whiskies, and bakers that actually
bake before breakfast. There are forests, too,
about Aberdeen, but the greatest are across the
deserted hills of what used to be Banff, on the
coastal plain of Moray, Roseisle, Culbin and
Speymouth.

And so to Inverness, where Culloden waits
to accuse you, or the Black Isle to soothe you,
and the high road spreads its long fingers to the
north and over the Kyle of Sutherland, to the
south-west down the Great Glen, or to the
western Highlands.

No ancient hardwoods survive to the east of
the Scottish Highlands. The oakwood at
Dinnet on Deeside is not of natural origin, and
the native trees at Loch of Lowes and
Hermitage do not add up to woodland. One
alderwood remains, at the Mound by Loch
Fleet, Sutherland. The high road, A9, crosses
it by a causeway, and it is swampy – besides
which, you need a permit. Perhaps you need go
no further than the bonny banks of Loch
Lomond, but you would miss a great deal of
truly wonderful scenery.

Key

The book is divided into sections which follow on numerically from west to east and south to north of the region. At the beginning of each section the relevant Ordnance Survey Landranger sheet numbers are listed. Each entry is headed with factual information in the form below:

            a   **b**   **c**

Burrator Forest *568 694*, ♀ ✿, *1000 acres, paths and a forest road, WA*

        d   **e**

a Ordnance Survey National Grid
    reference – usually of the nearest car park
b Type of woodland: ♀ deciduous
                  ♠ coniferous ✿ marsh
c Size of wooded area
d Type of walk
e Owner of site

How to find a grid reference

The reference for Burrator Forest is *568 694*
56 – Can be found in the top and bottom margins of the relevant map sheet (identified at the start of each book section). It is the reference number for one of the grid lines running north/south on the map.
69 – Can be found in the left and right hand margins of the relevant map sheet. It is the reference number for one of the grid lines running east/west on the map.

These numbers locate the bottom left hand corner of the kilometre grid square in which the car park for Burrator Forest appears. The remaining figures of the reference (*568 694*) pinpoint the feature within the grid square to the nearest 100 metres as shown in the diagram below.

The following abbreviations are used:

AONB Area of outstanding natural beauty
CNT *County Naturalists' Trust*
CP   Country Park
FC   Forestry Commission
FNR Forest Nature Reserve
fp   footpath
GLC Greater London Council
LA   Local Authority
LNR Local Nature Reserve
MAFF Ministry of Agriculture Fisheries and
         Food
NC   Nature Conservancy
NNR National Nature Reserve
NT   National Trust
NTS National Trust for Scotland
pf   private forestry
SSSI Site of Special Scientific Interest
SWT Scottish Wildlife Trust
WA   Water Authority
WT   Woodland Trust

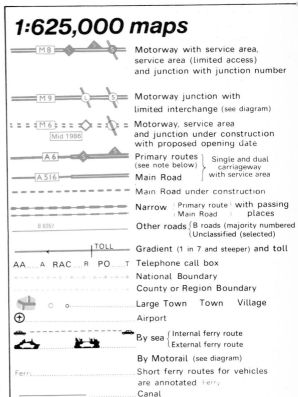

1:625,000 maps

M8	Motorway with service area, service area (limited access) and junction with junction number
M9	Motorway junction with limited interchange (see diagram)
M6 Mid 1986	Motorway, service area and junction under construction with proposed opening date
A6	Primary routes (see note below) } Single and dual carriageway with service area
A516	Main Road }
	Main Road under construction
	Narrow { Primary route } with passing { Main Road } places
B 6357	Other roads { B roads (majority numbered) { Unclassified (selected)
TOLL	Gradient (1 in 7 and steeper) and toll
AA....A RAC....R PO....T	Telephone call box
	National Boundary
	County or Region Boundary
	Large Town Town Village
⊕	Airport
	By sea { Internal ferry route { External ferry route
	By Motorail (see diagram)
Ferry	Short ferry routes for vehicles are annotated *Ferry*
	Canal
	Coastline, river and lake
427•	Height (metres)

The reference for Burrator Forest is *568 694*

```
     56                                    57
70 ──┼───────────────────────────────────┼── 70
     │                                     │
     │   Burrator Forest Parking ──→ ✕     │
     │                                     │
69 ──┼───────────────────────────────────┼── 69
     56        Grid reference 5669        57
```

The dotted lines within the square do not appear on the face of the map

1:316,800 maps

RELIEF

Feet	Metres	
		· 274
		Heights in feet above mean sea level
3000	914	
2000	610	
1400	427	
1000	305	Contours at 200ft intervals
600	183	
200	61	
		To convert feet to metres multiply by 0·3048
0	0	

TOURIST INFORMATION

- ✝ Abbey, Cathedral, Priory
- m Ancient monument
- 🐟 Aquarium
- ⚊ Camp site
- 🚐 Caravan site
- 🏰 Castle
- Cave
- 🏕 Country park
- 🎨 Craft centre
- ❀ Garden
- ⛳ Golf course or links
- 🏛 Historic house
- ℹ Information centre
- 🏁 Motor racing
- 🏛 Museum
- ! Nature or forest trail
- Nature reserve
- ☆ Other tourist feature
- ✕ Picnic site
- 🚂 Preserved railway
- 🏇 Racecourse
- ⛷ Skiing
- Viewpoint
- Wildlife park
- ▲ Youth hostel
- 🐘 Zoo

ROADS Not necessarily rights of way

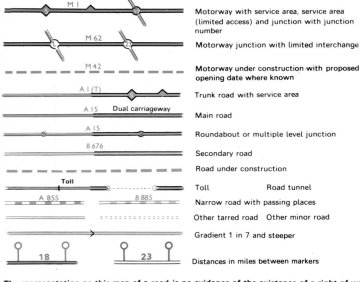

Motorway with service area, service area (limited access) and junction with junction number

Motorway junction with limited interchange

Motorway under construction with proposed opening date where known

Trunk road with service area

Main road

Roundabout or multiple level junction

Secondary road

Road under construction

Toll   Road tunnel

Narrow road with passing places

Other tarred road   Other minor road

Gradient 1 in 7 and steeper

Distances in miles between markers

The representation on this map of a road is no evidence of the existence of a right of way

GENERAL FEATURES

- Buildings
- Wood
- Lighthouse (in use)
- Lighthouse (disused)
- ✠ Windmill
- Radio or TV mast
- Youth hostel
- ⊕ Civil aerodrome { with Customs facilities
- ✛ Civil aerodrome { without Customs facilities
- Ⓗ Heliport
- ☎ Public telephone
- Motoring organisation telephone

ANTIQUITIES

- ✳ Native fortress
- Castle · Other antiquities
- ⚔ Site of battle (with date)
- Roman road (course of)
- CANOVIUM · Roman antiquity
- m Ancient Monuments and Historic Buildings in the care of the Secretaries of State for the Environment, for Scotland and for Wales and that are open to the public.

WATER FEATURES

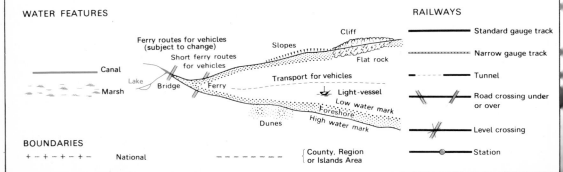

- Canal
- Lake
- Marsh
- Bridge
- Ferry
- Ferry routes for vehicles (subject to change)
- Short ferry routes for vehicles
- Transport for vehicles
- Slopes
- Cliff
- Flat rock
- Light-vessel
- Low water mark
- Foreshore
- High water mark
- Dunes

RAILWAYS

- Standard gauge track
- Narrow gauge track
- Tunnel
- Road crossing under or over
- Level crossing
- Station

BOUNDARIES

- + — · — · — · — National
- — — — — — { County, Region or Islands Area

1:50,000 maps

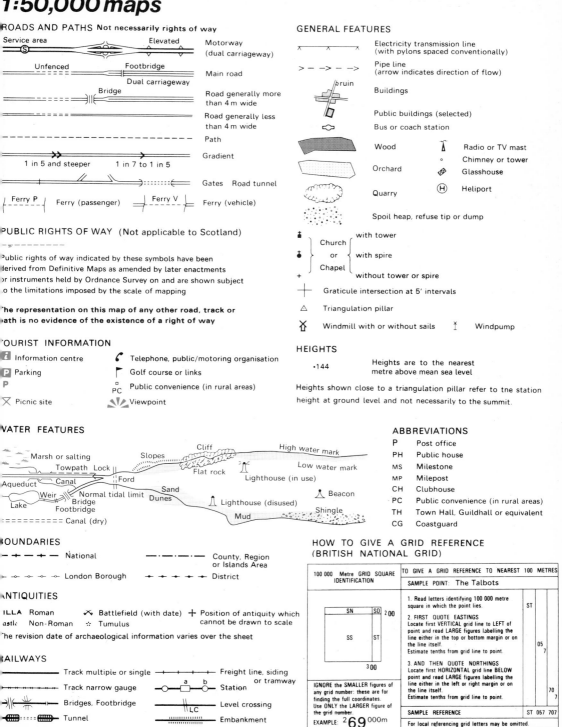

ROADS AND PATHS Not necessarily rights of way

Service area / Elevated	Motorway (dual carriageway)
Unfenced / Footbridge	Main road
Dual carriageway	
Bridge	Road generally more than 4 m wide
	Road generally less than 4 m wide
	Path
Gradient	
1 in 5 and steeper / 1 in 7 to 1 in 5	
Gates Road tunnel	
Ferry P Ferry (passenger) / Ferry V Ferry (vehicle)	

PUBLIC RIGHTS OF WAY (Not applicable to Scotland)

Public rights of way indicated by these symbols have been derived from Definitive Maps as amended by later enactments or instruments held by Ordnance Survey on and are shown subject to the limitations imposed by the scale of mapping

The representation on this map of any other road, track or path is no evidence of the existence of a right of way

TOURIST INFORMATION

i	Information centre		Telephone, public/motoring organisation
P	Parking		Golf course or links
P		PC	Public convenience (in rural areas)
✕	Picnic site		Viewpoint

WATER FEATURES

Marsh or salting
Towpath   Lock
Aqueduct   Canal
Weir   Normal tidal limit
Lake   Bridge
Footbridge
Canal (dry)

Slopes   Cliff   High water mark
Flat rock   Low water mark
Ford   Lighthouse (in use)
Sand   Dunes
Beacon
Lighthouse (disused)
Mud   Shingle

BOUNDARIES

	National		County, Region or Islands Area
	London Borough		District

ANTIQUITIES

VILLA Roman	✕ Battlefield (with date)	+ Position of antiquity which cannot be drawn to scale
Castle Non-Roman	☆ Tumulus	

The revision date of archaeological information varies over the sheet

RAILWAYS

	Track multiple or single		Freight line, siding or tramway
	Track narrow gauge		Station
	Bridges, Footbridge		Level crossing
	Tunnel		Embankment
	Viaduct		Cutting

GENERAL FEATURES

	Electricity transmission line (with pylons spaced conventionally)
	Pipe line (arrow indicates direction of flow)
bruin	Buildings
	Public buildings (selected)
	Bus or coach station
	Wood
	Orchard
	Quarry
	Spoil heap, refuse tip or dump

Radio or TV mast	
° Chimney or tower	
Glasshouse	
H Heliport	

Church or Chapel { with tower / with spire / without tower or spire }

Graticule intersection at 5' intervals

△   Triangulation pillar

Windmill with or without sails   Windpump

HEIGHTS

•144   Heights are to the nearest metre above mean sea level

Heights shown close to a triangulation pillar refer to the station height at ground level and not necessarily to the summit.

ABBREVIATIONS

P	Post office
PH	Public house
MS	Milestone
MP	Milepost
CH	Clubhouse
PC	Public convenience (in rural areas)
TH	Town Hall, Guildhall or equivalent
CG	Coastguard

HOW TO GIVE A GRID REFERENCE (BRITISH NATIONAL GRID)

100 000 Metre GRID SQUARE IDENTIFICATION	TO GIVE A GRID REFERENCE TO NEAREST 100 METRES
	SAMPLE POINT: The Talbots
SN / SO 200 / SS / ST / 300	1. Read letters identifying 100 000 metre square in which the point lies. ST
	2. FIRST QUOTE EASTINGS Locate first VERTICAL grid line to LEFT of point and read LARGE figures labelling the line either in the top or bottom margin or on the line itself. Estimate tenths from grid line to point. 05 7
	3. AND THEN QUOTE NORTHINGS Locate first HORIZONTAL grid line BELOW point and read LARGE figures labelling the line either in the left or right margin or on the line itself. Estimate tenths from grid line to point. 70 7
IGNORE the SMALLER figures of any grid number: these are for finding the full coordinates. Use ONLY the LARGER figure of the grid number.	
EXAMPLE: ²69 000m	SAMPLE REFERENCE ST 057 707
	For local referencing grid letters may be omitted.

Galloway and South Strathclyde

Landranger sheets
69, 70, 71, 77, 78, 83

The forest road, Ae

Columnar form of juniper at Tynron

DUMFRIES

Forest of Ae *982 912*, ♀, *about 30 sq m, forest walks, FC*

Ae is just an ordinary Scottish forest, one of many, but it is half as big as the New Forest. Nothing much happens there, except that spruces grow, and burns rush from the hills into the Water of Ae. By the water is a level, grassy place for picnicking, surrounded by some of the spruces – tall Norway spruce about forty years old. The two walks are easy, and reveal little more than does the drive in, about $1\frac{1}{2}$ miles up the river from Ae village. (Stop at the Forest Office here for a leaflet.) There is a longer, tougher Green Hills Trail. Pony trekking can be arranged, as at many Scottish centres.

Tynron Juniper Wood *828 927*, ♀ (♣), *15 acres, NNR*

Driving from Thornhill to Moniaive (pronounced Moanyive) on the A702 – do not turn off for Tynron village – the wood is on a hillside above the road, where a stream runs parallel on the other side.

Junipers are naturally decorative and take columnar or bushy form according to some law of their own. *Juniperus communis* is the most widely distributed tree of the north temperate zone, and the species ranges from North America to Russia, equally at home on chalk downs or in mountain valleys where it is a constituent of the Caledonian Pine Forest, among others. A dwarf form is found above the

tree-line in Scotland, and on windy limestone cliffs of the Gower Peninsula, for instance.

The wood looks a little tame from the road, perhaps – almost like a cemetery. But beware; this wood is not for walking in. A path leads around the top of the wood from the by-road which turns off uphill. There are picturesque ash and cherry trees as well, and broom on the slope with gorse below. Juniper berries take two years to ripen from green to their lovely grey-bloomed blue. The name of gin, a Dutch invention, comes from the berries formerly supplying the flavour, now achieved chemically. Only here at Tynron can you appreciate the beautiful striated bark of the trees. The timber is hard and fragrant.

The strip of land between the road and the wood looks a mess, and it is a pity that the farmer cannot either give it up or be a bit less careless with barbed wire and other equipment. Follow the road to Auchenbrack by Shinnel Water for bird cherry, white in June.

The Forestry Commission has provided picnic places in the **Mabie Forest**, *950 711*, with old sawmill shelter and four forest walks, and at **Dalbeattie Forest**, *836 600*, with walks on granite quarry tracks. On the coast here is the National Trust's complex of Rockcliffe and Rough Island, once remote settlements: luxuriant scrub on the Muckle lands now crossed by the Jubilee Path.

GALLOWAY FOREST PARK

Loch Ken is known for oak and alder woods. There are many stopping places on the western lochside, along the A762, and here is the eastern border of the Galloway Forest Park, 240 square miles of forests, moors, mountains and lochs, and the Raiders' Road.

Forest Drive: Raiders' Road *654 720 (Loch Ken) to 546 752 (Clatteringshaws)*, ♀ (♣), *12m, FC*

There is an automatic ticket machine at each end, if you happen to have the right change. The drive is really good value, especially at the south-east end where spruce is being extracted leaving fantastic great heaps of roots, and foxgloves. The Stroan Loch is beautiful. There are walks waymarked from here. Stands of trees are named, so that you can read as you flash by at a maximum 20 mph. There are plenty of places to stop, and by the Black Water of Dee there is a good bronze of an otter by Penny Wheatley which the children will love to see. But will it not frighten the otters, being more than lifesize? The name Raiders' Road comes from a novel by S. R. Crockett. Buchan's *The Thirty-Nine Steps* is also set in Galloway.

Stroan Loch

Clatteringshaws *552 765*

The name is so resounding that the 1900s' brutalist architecture of the dam comes as a shock. However, the view, over the great stony-margined lake, of the Rhinns of Kells and the Merrick (when visible), is unimpeded. The National Trust for Scotland looks after a boulder on which Robert the Bruce leaned in 1307, now nicely surrounded by Scots pines instead of dead Englishmen, and the Forestry Commission has a deer museum: neat, clean, informative, deserted and warm. Down the road is the Deer Range with a viewpoint and a hide for hire.

Towards Newton Stewart on the A712 is a wild goat park and Murray's Monument. Murray was a shepherd's son who became a professor – you get a monument for that? **Talnotry** is a class B campsite, and there is a forest trail, *487 716*, of rough walking for 4 miles over uneven but interesting country. The leaflet, said to be essential, comes from the camp shop or other Forestry Commission offices. It was raining very hard and I didn't stop.

A mini survey of a small glen at about 1000 ft above Moniaive revealed the trees whose leaves are shown here, photographed on a sheet of A2 paper. The beech (centre) and ash (bottom right) may have been planted to shelter a habitation now ruined. The hawthorn (top right) and the two sallows (bottom left) share the burnside with the wych elm (top left), the dominant and only native timber tree here. Most of the Scottish wych elms – it can be called the Scottish elm – have escaped Dutch elm disease.

NEWTON STEWART

Kirroughtree Forest, which includes the campsite mentioned above, also has a forest garden walk, $\frac{1}{2}$ mile, which includes sixty tree species. Three miles south-east of Newton Stewart on the A75(T) to Gatehouse turn off at Palnure. The picnic site, *451 646*, is a little exposed but pleasant, by a village that is quiet in the way only a Scottish village can be. The neat, grey school now functions as an 'education centre' and the Forestry Commission provides a forest schoolroom with, amongst other things, a useful collection of rock samples.

Wood of Cree *382 708*, ♀ ♠, *200 acres approx, fp and forest road, RSPB*
The Galloway Forest Park appears now to extend down the Cree to include at least part of this oakwood. Cross the Cree Bridge in Newton Stewart and take the minor road up the east bank by Minnigaff, turning left over the burn, leaving the church on your right. The road, bordered here and there by beautiful oak coppice, appears to strike out into the moors but in fact soon rejoins the Cree.

Numerous streams pour down the steep, oak-covered banks, forming dark pools where rowans hopefully spread their delicate branches. The oaks, sessile of course, make a continuous pattern constantly varied by their wayward coppiced trunks, over a ground flora

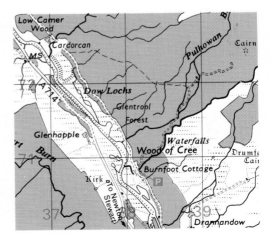

Field layer of cow wheat beneath the oaks of the Wood of Cree

which itself varies from bilberry to cow wheat to grass or honeysuckle, with patches of bluebell. There are very occasional birches. Such a large area of ancient oak coppice is a rarity anywhere and it should be highly valued.

The path, along a forest road or cart track, winds upwards from the parking place with a few larger oaks and some ash, to a rougher, heathy, boggy top (some sweetgale) with heaps of stones and some ruinous houses which are fenced off. A bridleway continues north-west down to Cardorcan, a caravan camp, joining the road $1\frac{1}{4}$ miles upstream from the car park. The road is not busy and you pass a beautiful waterfall on the way back.

Loch Trool *416 803 (Bruce Memorial), 399 789 (Caldons Wood),* ♀ *(♠), various walks, FC*
Interest in the region centres on the Glentrool Forest; and the loch itself, narrow, serpentine and, one imagines, mysteriously deep under the slope of Merrick (2764 feet), is to me in a class of its own. It is always still and dark,

certainly dark when compared with the much more remote lochs of the wilderness above. These have no forests but are not without trees and have white beaches. From one of these I was tempted once to bathe for a freezing minute, never to be repeated.

The Bruce Memorial at Loch Trool is decently below the skyline and is a good viewpoint. A trail all round the loch starts at the Caldons Wood campsite, entailing a rather embarrassing circuit of people's tents before starting a $4\frac{1}{2}$ mile tramp partly through oakwood remnants of the ancient forest. These are also evident on the short walk to the Martyrs' Tomb, where the six martyrs were 'surprised in this house by Colnel Douglas, Lieutnant Livingston and Cornet James Douglas and by them most impiously and cruely murthured for their adherence to Scotland's reformation ...', 1685. The oaks here are beautiful trees.

Another trail goes back along the glen already traversed by road, and there is a stiff walk up the Merrick from the Bruce Stone –

Oak trunks: in the Wood of Cree (left) and at the Martyrs' Tomb

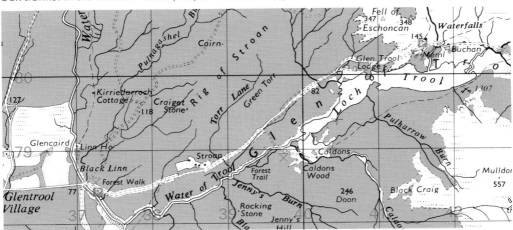

but only for experienced hill walkers.

It was late, and I had only time to pay my respects to the martyrs before the midges made life impossible. There are three ways of dealing with Highland midges, and these do not include ultrasonic devices or insect repellents. One is to keep moving, a hard discipline after a long day; two is to make a very smoky fire and to sit in the smoke; three, and most effective, is to get indoors and to stay there.

North of the Merrick and approached by Straiton there are two forest walks: a hill walk and the Stinchar Falls Walk from Stinchar Bridge car park, *396 956*. There are picnic places at Tairlaw Toll, 5 miles south of

In Lambdoughty Glen

Straiton, and Changue, near Barr on the B734. Fishing is the main preoccupation here, details from the Forestry Commission, Sraiton.

Culzean Castle 246 100, ♀ ♣, 560 acres, easy walks, NTS, CP

The z is silent. There is a fairly heavy charge to take your car in, justified by the amenities available, and the restoration of the Robert Adam farm buildings as the Park Centre, not to mention the upkeep of the superlatively fine castle and its gardens. Walkers may enter at various points: north of Maidens on the coast, at Morriston off the A719 and at Kennels Mount, 242 097. An old railway track which skirts the policies runs from Maidens north-east to Dunure, and is a right-of-way for walkers.

Two pleasant, partly shaded picnic places present themselves as you drive into the main castle car park. You can take your car on, to the Deer Park (herd on view) and Walled Garden or to the Swan Pond, a mile from the centre. The Happy Valley Wood, roughly south of the Walled Garden and east of the Swan Pond, is the home of some remarkable conifers, grouped most informally and closely integrated with lesser vegetation. Lawson cypresses have amazing sweeping lower limbs, after 130 years of growth, and there are old Nootka cypress, Sitka spruce, Douglas fir, hemlock and *Sequoiadendron*. Chusan palms are well grown but look unhappy. A gardener's trick of growing rambler roses up tall deciduous trees is effective near the Camellia House.

Fine silvery beeches are perhaps the most attractive woodland feature in spite of the exotics.

Lambdoughty Glen, Straiton 392 052, ♀ ♣, 22 acres, ¾ hour walk, pf

The modest joys of Lady Hunter Blair's walk have been available to all since 1840, a gesture of the 3rd Baronet of Blairquhan in memory of his wife. There are two linns, one with a Leyland cypress, and the other named after the poet Rossetti, who, staying nearby, came and contemplated suicide by drowning – too many

Morning mist on the River Nith near Sanquhar

bannocks perhaps. Linn, the equivalent of the Welsh *llyn*, means pool, but is applied to falls which of course create pools. Sitka spruce is planted in the glen, and the leaflet, price two pence, on sale at the minute car park, reminds us that Britain spends more than £3000 million a year importing timber. The monument on the nearby hill is to Colonel James Hunter Blair, killed in the Crimea.

As you drive north-eastwards through the fine, empty-feeling lowland and upland pastures, lines of beeches, not quite as silvery as at Culzean, are conspicuous, planted as shelter-belts or grown up from hedges. Why beech? I suppose the answer is why not? It was a well-tried favourite hardwood of policy plantations, and although it is often said in Scotland that it

was imported from England, the beech is in fact a native Scottish tree and was growing in the eastern lowlands when the Romans got there. When most of the trees were planted, the glens were still full of oak, birch and alder, as indeed many of them still are. Anyway, they brighten the place up no end.

A desert intervenes between Upper Nithsdale, where, on the heights, people are content to live in concrete huts and keep bulls, and Clydesdale. But even the Upper Nith has moments of beauty. The desert was broken for me by the beautiful valley of the Crawick Water traversed by the B740. The town of Douglas is well wooded and in fine country, but the Forestry Commission's Douglas Forest has no apparent access, only a connection with the nature reserve below.

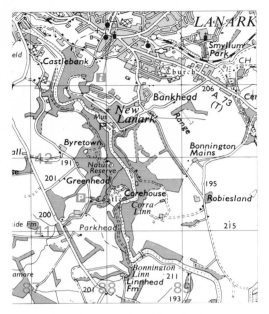

Lanark: Falls of the Clyde

878 415 (west bank), 881 423 (New Lanark), ♀ ♣, 2m of fps on each bank, pf, NR, FC

The upper falls, Bonnington Linn, were the subject of a large early watercolour by Turner (now at Port Sunlight) in which his bathing beauties, I was disappointed to find, were pygmies, making the falls look twice as high. The walk from here to the lower Corra Linn is largely an auditory experience, though glimpses of authentic oak and alder boscage can be got through the invading sycamores and inevitable spruces. At Corra Linn the view broadens and one cannot fail to be impressed. There are great trees here by the ruined Corra Castle, and the water shoots forward with enormous force and sound, native trees projecting themselves horizontally into the mist. It was depressing to have to clear several items of discarded food packaging before taking a photograph from the rocks.

The nature reserve has a total of 127 acres on both banks, with a Visitors' Centre and warden in New Lanark. I am delighted to read that the woodland is being converted gradually to broadleaves. There are supposed to be kingfishers and otters, but the whole affair is a bit too close to Lanark for comfort, not that I've got anything against Lanark. A power station in concrete, cathedral style, is just below Corra, and is organized to divert the water that it needs from the falls, sometimes all of it.

Island of Arran

Arran Forest has two Forestry Commission picnic sites; off the A841, 2 miles south of Brodick, *017 343*, and off the Ross road, *012 297*, ½ mile from Lamlash Bay. The National Trust for Scotland has Brodick Castle, its garden, Country Park and woodland walk, and Goat Fell, 603 acres; 40,000 visitors a year.

Kintyre: Carradale Forest

Carradale Forest's information point is at *803 382*.

Scottish bluebells by the Falls of Clyde

SCOTLAND
The Border Forests

Landranger sheets 72, 73, 79, 80

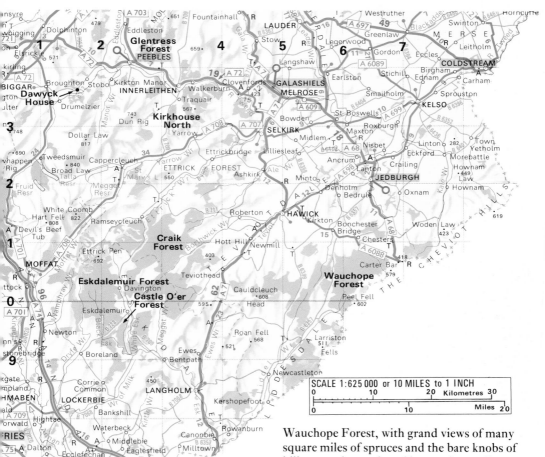

Wauchope Forest, with grand views of many square miles of spruces and the bare knobs of hills around 1500 feet. Above a deep valley, which could be in Norway or Canada, or even Switzerland, is the pine-shaded site of Piet's Nest, a few picnic benches with a view to the north of Rubers Law, 1392 feet. Piet's Nest is a high, quiet place, not much frequented and with no irritating facilities.

Wauchope Forest 586 052 (Piet's Nest),
♠, picnic place, FC
Driving northwards from Kielder village soon brings you to the Scottish border, marked by a plain notice and an improved Scottish road surface (a pretentious heraldic sign for England if you are coming south). A right turn on to the B6357 takes you climbing to the

Craik Forest 349 082 (Craik village), ♠,
forest walks, $1\frac{1}{2}$ and 3m, FC
The B711 west from busy Hawick has wonderful views over Teviotdale. Craik, a forest village, is signposted on a No Through Road, 8 miles of it, along Borthwick Water, in

Wauchope Forest from Piet's Nest

a rich, lovely valley with many ancient settlements. The parking place is in the tiny village with a picnic place beyond and walks in the forest – to Wolfcleuchhead Waterfall, 3 miles total, or a short circuit; or, if you feel like it, 8 miles due south to Eskdalemuir. **Eskdalemuir Forest** is large and abuts onto Castle O'er Forest, which has a picnic place near the Black Esk River, off the B723, not marked on the 1975 OS 1:50,000 map.

The B711 passes by Alemoor Loch and alongside a broad arm of the Craik Forest, where the young trees share the uplands with herds of sheep and cattle, and all is quiet and dignified.

NORTH-EAST OF CRAIK FOREST

If you go by St Mary's Loch (A708) then north by the B709 you come to a charming picnic place, *315 317*, planted with grey alders, and

Looking over Teviotdale

provided for the public by the **Kirkhouse North Estate**, in memory of John Parker, MP, a great tree man. You are invited to walk and not to leave litter. It is not clear exactly where you walk – much has been clear-felled – but the footpath goes through a pretty birchwood before disappearing. Climb to the forest road to explore further. A few feet of elevation here brings a richly rewarding view.

As for litter, you'd hardly believe that people would throw things into this lovely stream, but they do.

By Peebles the **Cardrona Forest**, Forestry Commission, offers a walk from a quiet parking place, and at Kailzie is an open-air restaurant, surely a brave venture: the view across the trees is really beautiful on a fine evening. Here the Forestry Commission's **Glentress Forest** parking place is a bit public, *285 399*, and threatened by a large tank within 20 feet of which no naked flames are to be used: but there is a picnic place up in the woods on one of the four trails, which include a short walk 'for the less energetic'. East towards Galashiels, the Forestry Commission's Ashiestiel Bridge walk was fouled up temporarily by pipe-laying works, but there is a viewpoint at The Nest, *433 354*, above the Tweed, with a painting in oils and pokerwork to help identify landmarks.

Round about Peebles the beeches take on an iron grey, as if in mediaeval armour, but in the less busy part of the Tweed Valley between the A701 and A72, near Stobo, they shine once again. Well they might, for at Dawyck House emerged the Dawyck beech, in 1860.

Dawyck Arboretum *163 353*, ♀ ♣, *Royal Botanic Garden, Edinburgh*

The Dawyck beech is a fastigiate form very like the Lombardy poplar, but nicer. There is a beech walk here too, the woods of surpassing beauty with silver firs and pines as well. Choose a fine day and go by Policy Bank, with large, perfect examples of such rare beauties as Armand's pine *Tsuga mertensiana*, *Picea breweriana* and *jezoensis*, *Calocedrus decurrens*, *Chamaecyparis nootkatensis* 'Pendula'. Firs are *Abies veitchii, homolepis, magnifica, mariesii*; and lesser, but there, *delavayi* and *concolor*, one

Silverwood beeches, Dawyck

with the lovely silver spine along the shoot, the other with wide-spaced, lax and slightly clammy bright green leaves.

Above to the south-west are large Douglas firs, and on a sweep of lawn by the chapel very large Sitka spruce and strangely naked-trunked *Picea orientalis*. Here a Douglas fir is unusually spreading and clumsy, and enormously thick in the trunk.

The house, vague but decent in style, with its good lawns surrounded by crumbling, grey urns, contrasted with a field of mown hay beyond, and surrounded by these magnificent trees, looked the essence of peace and security in the late-afternoon sun. I must admit that I stood on the Policy Bank with tears in my eyes. Well, thank goodness the National Trust for Scotland didn't get it: at least it is still dedicated – no longer to its privileged Naesmyth owners but to the science of botany and the art of gardening. It could all have been built up only by a rich and sensitive man. Nothing as good is likely to emerge during the next 2000 years. We are lucky to have the means to discover such places in the brief interval before they have to be cocooned in silicone, to protect them from the hazards of mass scrutiny. The house is private, the gardens open daily.

SCOTLAND
South Argyll and Loch Lomond

Landranger sheets 55, 56, 57, 58, 62, 63, 64, 68

ARGYLL FOREST PARK

Britain's first Forest Park was established in 1935, ten years before any English National Park, and covers 100 square miles, with 165 miles of forest roads open to walkers. Older stands of spruce, sea lochs and great mountains are its features, but there are several notable arboreta within the Forest Park and gardens.

Ardgartan Forest

The north of the Argyll Forest Park has its centre at Ardgartan, *275 030*, with a Forestry Commission campsite (class A) and fairly tough walking, waymarked in colours, from 3 to 12 miles. Shorter walks can of course be worked out. There is a Forestry Commission guide to the Forest Park. A small arboretum is at Lochgoilhead, near the Forest Office.

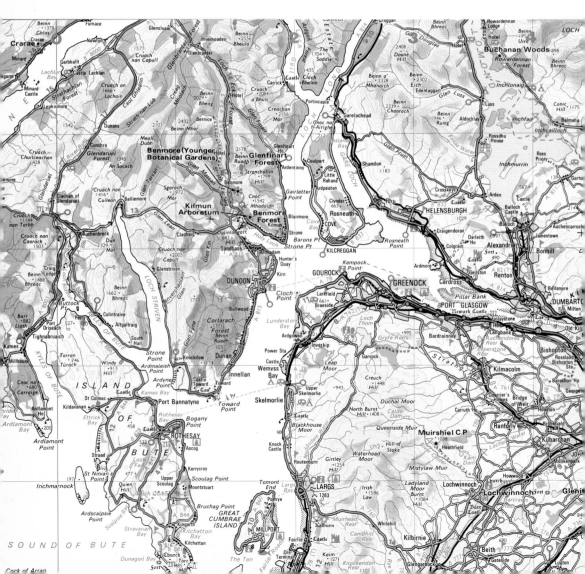

Benmore Forest *192 886 (Finart Bay, Ardentinny), 2 walks, fairly stiff, FC*
The forest around Kilmun Hill and the shores of Loch Long is picturesque, being largely of old-established Norway spruce and in a magnificent setting. The picnic place given is on the sandy beach of Loch Long. Small roads cross and parking is not a problem as long as you keep your back wheels out of drainage channels. The walk from Ardentinny to Carrick Castle, 5 miles north, starts from the picnic place. A walk, Black Gates to Puck's Glen, starts near the parking ground, *144 854,*

for Benmore Arboretum and either doubles back to it or continues to Puck's Glen, as you choose.

The road, the A815, runs for 10 miles along the east shore of Loch Eck and gives access to a wide range of woodland. The Loch Eck Forest is productive, but the forestry is mixed, and trees flourish by the waterside. The glen, running north to south, and sheltered by 2000-foot mountainsides, is a world apart, with its own weather, usually wet, always mild – and unforgettable when the sun does come out.

There is a Forestry Commission picnic place

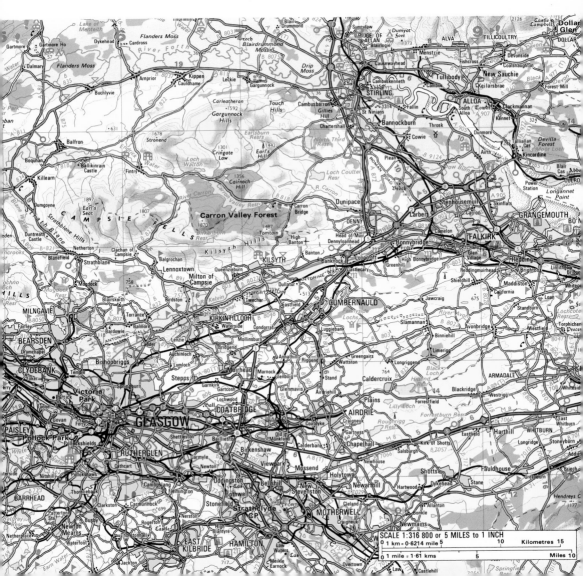

SCALE 1:316 800 or 5 MILES to 1 INCH

A September morning, Loch Eck

Benmore Forest, Argyll

at the side of Loch Eck. This, and Glen Finart, are part of the Commission's Benmore Forest, which is itself part of the Argyll Forest Park. A guidebook is available for the 165 miles of forest roads which are open to walkers.

Inverary Castle Gardens, *096 093*, have great conifers, with grand firs over 150 feet, and Leyland cypress planted in the late 1920s approximately 100 feet high. The gardens are open seasonally.

Benmore (Younger Botanical Gardens) *144 854, ♀ ♣, 56 acres arboretum, 2 suggested walks, Royal Botanic Garden, Edinburgh*

The Younger Botanical Gardens surround Benmore House, now a hostel, and fittingly commemorate the gesture of H. G. Younger in presenting the great Benmore estate to the nation. His predecessor, James Duncan, planted 6,488,000 trees in this valley, creating a forest of 1622 acres.

The ferry from Gourock to Dunoon costs more than a pound a minute, but the alternative is an 80-mile drive from Glasgow. As you enter the gardens (open daily from April to October) you cross the swift River Eachaig and are at once between two lines of giant *Sequoiadendron*, raising their saps to 130 feet or more – a disturbing opposition of watery forces to those sensitive to such things. But the trees, like the many other tall conifers here, are dwarfed by the cloud-topped mountains. By the house are some large and particularly opulent *Araucaria*. The warm, moist atmosphere of this region suits all the firs, and there is a Chinese Fir Garden at the extreme south-west of the arboretum. Here you will find the only mature specimens in the

28

country of Delavay's fir, and beautiful they are, with thick, low-sweeping branches flashing streaks of white as you move around them. Only varieties of this tree are known elsewhere in Britain. Beyond a group of very tall Douglas firs you may glimpse the spires of two *Abies amabilis*, the beautiful fir, their trunks nearly white, subtly marked, one or two wounds revealing a deep salmon pink. The (orange-scented) foliage is out of reach above the rhododendrons. Nearer to the house are large Scots pines planted in 1820, and the largest *Tsuga heterophylla*, western hemlock, in Britain, 160 feet.

Besides the invariably well-grown conifers, there are old and young broadleaved trees, *Nothofagus* among them, a small and a large katsura, and several very healthy Hupeh rowans, a favourite here. There are 250 species of rhododendron, for most of which you have to climb the hillside above the house. This is the longer of two walks recommended in the booklet, which has pleasant photographs and a useless map. On the flat, in autumn, a particularly fine *Eucryphia* blooms near the pond and a small Cappadocian maple gleams pure gold under the *Sequoiadendron*, the blue hills of Glen Eck beyond.

Kilmun Arboretum *165 822,* ♀ ♣, *200 acres, 3 suggested walks, FC*

Kilmun Arboretum is free and open all the year round. The approximately rectangular plots date from about 1930 and 1950, hung precipitously over the Holy Loch at what feels like 45 degrees or more to the horizontal. The climb is hard but worth every puff of it, if only for the view which is not spoilt – but perhaps it ought to be – by the American submarine supply ships in the loch.

Two groups of *Eucalyptus* plots can be reached easily from the forest road which runs at a gentle gradient from the south-east (church) entrance. The forest plots as a whole contain the widest selection of eucalyptus to be seen in Britain. Most of the trees are about thirty years old. Since this is unique I will point out one or two species. You can find the fruits of *Eucalyptus urnigera*, the urn-fruited gum, and admire the decorative trunks of

Eucalyptus gigantea at Kilmun

E. dalrympleana, the broadleaved kindling bark and *E. gigantea*, the gum-top stringy bark. There are black and broadleaved sallees; the name sallee comes from England. Black sally is still the name of the grey sallow in Oxfordshire. Besides the more familiar *E. perriniana* (round-leaved snow gum or spinning gum) and *E. gunnii* (the cider gum), several others have done very well, *E. simmondsii*, for instance, with clusters of button-like fruit, and *E. vernicosa* sp. *columnaris*, grown 70 feet since 1949. According to the leaflet available from the Forest Office at the central car park, there were another dozen planted in 1969. The very efficient labels, giving source and date of planting, are only sometimes broken or missing.

Nearly all Kilmun's specimens are in plots of about $\frac{1}{4}$ acre, which means that one is usually looking at a wood of a single species. It is worthwhile to climb right to the top, where at 1000 feet the ground begins to level out and an open patch of Sitka spruce reveals an unexpected poetry in this overworked species. The views are terrific, if the weather is fine. From these high levels you can zig-zag downwards to see the trees of your choice. Oldish plantations of *Tsuga* on the south-east side are very impressive; dark interiors, heavily curtained edges in the richest of dark greens. See the healthy-looking wood of *Abies pindro* (west Himalayan fir) and the extraordinary young *Abies lasiocarpa* var. 'Arizonica', the Alpine or cork-barked fir of a quite remarkable blue. This fir is very rare in Britain. Next to it, the plot of *Abies amabilis*, the beautiful fir, looked more businesslike than beautiful.

There are paperbark birches (looking a bit damp and grey), lovely, shiny barked, young, grey alders (in the south-east) and red oaks and southern beeches (north-west). There are plots of monkey puzzles and dawn redwoods. Distrust the printed sketch map. Where it laconically notes 'cherry' I found a sycamore, Norway maple, a pinaster pine, planes, walnuts, hickory, Armand's pine and white spruce.

Kilmun, though designed for pure forestry purposes, is full of a sort of wildness and has an invigorating aura. You will be tired at the end of a day there, but you can hardly fail to love the place. And if you have a few acres, or yards, of Scotland to plant with trees, Kilmun can provide excellent guidance.

Crarae 990 976, ♀ ♣, *pathways and 'circular pathways', 800 yds to 1m, open daily, pf*

Crarae Woodland Garden has been built up over eighty years; so quickly do great trees grow here that only one original survives, a *Thuja plicata*, western red cedar, 106 feet high, near the Crarae Burn below the house (Crarae Lodge). There are dozens of notable trees of which I will single out *Nothofagus dombeyi* and

Crarae, the Woodland Garden

Eucalyptus coccifera, which the previous owner, Sir Ilay Campbell Bt, describes as the most striking tree in the garden. Low cloud attended my visit, and I was more struck by the *Nothofagus*, deliciously lichened and enormous. Conifers are varied in interest from a picturesque leaning *Pinus radiata* – of immense proportions and absolutely covered in old cones – to youngish silver firs, Honda and tiger tail spruces, Korean pine, Macedonian pine. There are attractive and vigorous birch plantations and many incidental beauties; hybrid poplars and 'exotic' maples among them. You can, of course, ignore the species altogether and enjoy a beautifully shaped garden, with a footbridge over the miniature

Birch and sallow by Loch Awe

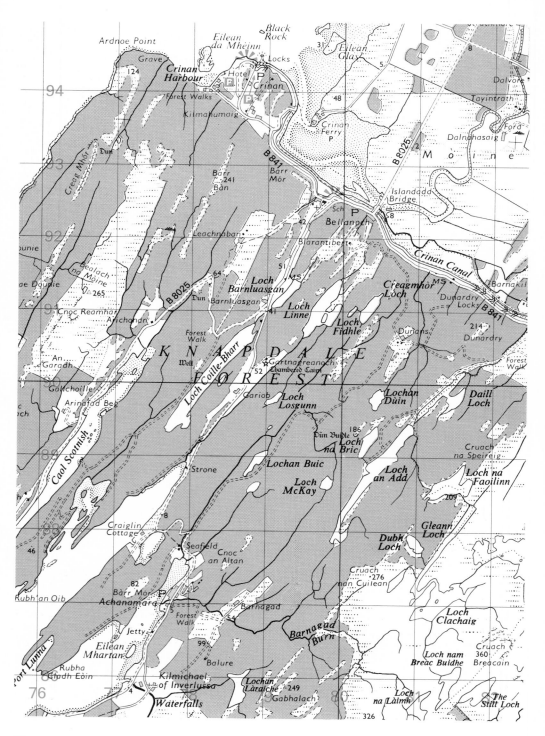

Ardnoe Point

Eilean
da Mheinn

Black
Rock

Grave

Locks

Eilean
Glas

Crinan
Harbour

124

Hotel

Crinan

Forest Walks

Kilmahumaig

Crinan
Ferry
P

Moine

Dalvore

Tayintrath

Ford

Dalnahasaig

Creag Mhòr

Dun

B 847

Barr
Mór

Islandadd
Bridge

Barr
Ban

241

Leachnaban

Blarantibert

Crinan Canal

Barnakill

ounie

ae Douie

Bealach
na Mòine

265

Cnoc Reamhar

Anchohan

B 8025

51

Loch
Barnluasgan

MS

Loch
Linne

Loch
Fidhle

Barnluasgan

Creagmhòr
Loch

Dunardry
Locks

B 847

214

Dunardry

Dun

Dunans

K N A P D A L E

An
Garadh

Loch Coille-Bharr

Well

52

Gartnagreanoch
Chambered Cairn

F O R E S T

Forest
Walk

Gallchoille

Arinafad Beg

Gariob

Loch
Losgunn

Lochan
Dùin

Daill
Loch

Caol Scotnish

Strone

Lochan Buic

Dun Bugle

186

Loch
na Bric

Cruach
na Speireig

Loch
an Add

Loch na
Faoilinn

Loch
McKay

209

Craiglin
Cottage

8

Gleann
Loch

46

Seafield

Cnoc
an Altan

Dubh
Loch

Cruach
nan Cuilean

276

Loch
Clachaig

Rubh' an Oib

82

Barr Mór

Achanamara

Barndgad

Barnagad
Burn

Cruach
Breacain

360

Forest
Walk

99

Loch nam
Breac Buidhe

Port Lunna

Jetty

Eilean
Mhartan

Balure

Rubha
Gladh Eòin

4

Kilmichael
of Inverlussa

Lochan
Làraiche

249

Gabhalach

Loch
na Làimh

The
Still Loch

Waterfalls

326

Oakwood on the east shore of Loch Lomond

gorge of the burn and many pleasant places to
stop. The forest garden to the north has an
uncertain future since the Forestry
Commission Research Branch made
it redundant. There are no labels in the
woodland garden to help identify specimens.

On the east side of Loch Awe the little road,
the B840, reveals many native trees decorated
with lichens: wych elm, alder, cherry, birch
and sallow, with chestnut and sycamore. There
are National Nature Reserve oakwoods beyond
in Glen Nant and at Glasdrum.

WESTERN FORESTS

For the more adventuresome the A83
continues to the Forests of Kilmichael,
Knapdale, Carradale and Arran. Information
about Knapdale Forest walks can be got from
the Forest District Office, Whitegates,
Lochgilphead.

At Taynish *725 830*, on the test bank of
Loch Sween, is one of the largest remaining
Scottish oakwoods, 800 acres, NNR.

LOCH LOMOND

All things come to an end, and a great glacier
which flowed and scraped its way from Ben
Lomond southwards eventually melted when it
had made a trough large enough to contain
93,000 million cu ft of water. How many frosty
winters and slightly less frosty summers it took
to do this I cannot compute, but it left us the
largest lake in Britain, then open to the sea.
After the melting of the ice, the land, relieved
of its load, rose sufficiently to separate the loch
from the sea. It is now a few feet above sea-
level and contains a fish, the powan, once
marine, that adapted to life in freshwater here
and in Loch Eck, and nowhere else.

The wide southern shores of Loch Lomond
are sandy, gravelly or stony with the remains of
the sea-shore and the terminal moraine, while
the upper, northern part, deeply excavated as
far as 600 feet, has steep sides of pre-Cambrian
rock. The natural vegetation of all the shores is
a rich woodland of alder, birch and oak, with
oak dominant, and with rowan and hazel up to
500 feet above the water – and further on the

33

Birch on Lomondside

Birch wood is not prized as a fine cabinet maker's material – it used to be used for cotton reels – but in the Highlands it has been used to make everything from beds to spoons. It is preferred for smoking herrings.

Two hard, dry bracket fungi are found on birch stems: surgeon's agaric – the powder was a dressing – and the razor strop fungus shown here in Morrone Birkwood. Both can be used as tinder.

banks of streams. The woods contain and support a rich and varied bird population.

The oaks were used and neglected, cut for charcoal and fuel and then grazed by cattle and goats – the surest way to get rid of woodland – until the middle of the eighteenth century, when the demand for oak bark for tannin increased. Remaining oaks – 1800 acres in the Buchanan Woods particularly – were coppiced. Most of the woods, however, were replanted, using broom, pine and larch as nurses for oak, sometimes with beech, ash and sycamore. Latterly, the Forestry Commission has acquired the Buchanan Woods, which include much of East Lomondside. Ben Lomond is now owned by the National Trust for Scotland. Rowardennan is the name of 15 square miles of Buchanan Woods which border with the old oakwood of Buchanan at the southern corner.

From Balmaha, *421 909*, to Rowardennan Lodge, *359 993*, where there is a Forestry Commission campsite (class A), footpaths go on for many miles north along the shore and east as far as Loch Ard.

The little motor road, which sometimes cuts through rock and slate, is in great contrast with its snarling, overloaded counterpart on the west bank. There are four main parking places.

Buchanan Woods *380 958 (Sallochy)*, ♀, *1¼m and ¾m, FC*

The shores of the loch in summer usually expose the roots of alders which have lost their soil and support the trunks well above the pebbles – an extraordinary effect as of mangroves which achieve the same effect in reverse by sending down roots from floating stations. A few yards inland, the oakwoods are full of character, with their history of coppicing, their banks gleaming with cow wheat. The walks are laid out, one by 'ancient routes of iron smelters, slate quarriers, foresters and crofters, passing through the ruined township of Wester Sallochy and another to Sunny Bay by the bonny banks of the Loch'.

There are two walks from Balmaha, gentle and steep – 'gentle' embraces a range of forest scenery. A lochside ring walk, very short, enables one to review the scenery from a car park, *405 927*, 1½ miles north of Balmaha.

From Balmaha you can visit the nature-reserve island of Inchcailloch. Here is a nature trail of 2½ miles, said to be one of the finest woodland walks in Scotland. 624 acres of Loch Lomond including five wooded islands and the marshy shore by Endrick Water are a National Nature Reserve. The islands are said to contain the best of Scotland's oakwoods – that is, least grazed and with the richest flora. Two small islands, Bucinch, which is wooded and with yews, and Ceardach, are the property of the National Trust for Scotland.

The Country Park of Balloch Castle at the south end of the loch, *395 830*, has a nature trail, shelters for wet-day picnics and fine grounds with views of Ben Lomond.

GLASGOW

In Glasgow there are no less than ten nature trails – for information telephone Glasgow 221 7371/2. Victoria Park, *538 675*, Scotstoun (Dunbarton Road, A814), fortified on two sides

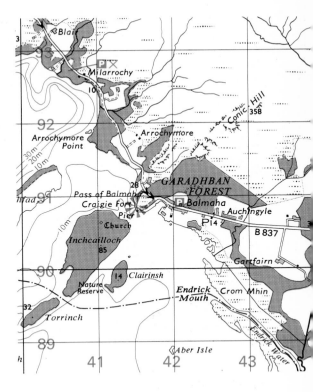

against the fast traffic, has the strangest woodland walk of all: a fossil forest in a Victorian shelter. It is well worth seeing, particularly as the park has beautiful trees: Cornish elms probably now gone, massive beeches, pretty Japanese maples, whitebeam and lime avenues.

Pollock Park, *555 625*, is now famous for containing the Burrel Collection of very expensive bric-à-brac in a well-designed 'woodland museum'.

Country Parks at Muirshiel, *319 628*, in the remote Calder Valley and Gleniffer Braes, *450 608*, south-west of Paisley have woodland, and the great Strathclyde Country Park, *735 572*, of 1601 acres, the third largest in Britain, has everything, with the M74 through the middle. At Lochwinnoch, *354 585*, is a large RSPB reserve, with some woodland, on the west bank of Aird Meadow.

North-east towards Stirling is the **Carron Valley Forest**. Forestry Commission picnic places are at Spittal Bridge – a winner this, on a river island breached by stepping stones, with safe paddling, *723 839*, at the eastern end of the reservoir; and at Sir John De Graham's Castle (who ever heard of anyone called Sir John De Graham, I ask you?) just east of Gartcarron.

Dollar Glen *965 986*, ♀, *1½m, steep paths,* NTS

'Dolour' it must be surely, where the Burn of Sorrow, flowing interminably, has cut deep into the rocks. Castle Campbell glooms above, while fairly well-to-do bungalows on Gloom Hill gaze across at Bank Hill. There is a nice oakwood on the Gloom side. The younger residents here have fought back, and installed a prize-winning outdoor gymnasium in the town field at the foot of the glen. Here the footpath up to the castle begins, with a warning to the unfit that the climb is steep. It isn't *too* bad, and, with well-maintained steps, walkways and footbridges, there is no rock scrambling to do.

The way is scattered with empty crisp, peanut and sweet packets, but the glen is filled with the richest of foliage, and the rocks hung with ferns and moss. The walk is so intricately laid out between the rocks and even under them as to be almost a caricature of the Grotesque. Dollar Glen is the countryside equivalent of the ghost train at the fair, and people, lots of them, come for thrills rather than to admire the trees. Still, it *is* beautiful.

In Dollar Glen

Lothian, Dunbar and Duns

Landranger sheets 58, 65, 66, 67

EDINBURGH

Within the city, the Royal Botanic Garden, *244 754*, is worth anyone's time. A gallery of modern art is at the top of the round hill, which is swathed in trees like an embroidered crinoline. I noted some really good oriental white birches and, working upwards, good exotic oaks, ashes and a sculpture I thought at first was some sort of civil-engineering installation or a squash court. At the top are *Sorbus* among others, very clean barked for the middle of a city, with a Marino Marini sculpture like an untutu'd Degas dancer, going a bit grey. In the gardens below are interesting crabs, many quite edible, and hawthorns, amongst them *Crataegus crus-gallii*, the cockspur thorn. There is a surprising sweep of heathers and conifers, miniature ones giving an illusion of perspective against the taller versions – surely a clever use of these over-used garden dwarfs. A fine luminous weeping willow is by the lake, and there is more to see beyond – walled gardens and glasshouses.

Within 9 miles of the centre of Edinburgh is a trio of Country Parks, all perhaps showing a leaning towards golf and water sports but still worthwhile attempts to make trees and plants accessible to all.

In West Lothian are **Beecraigs**, *008 743*, 793 acres, old forestry land and the reservoir a bird sanctuary, and **Almondale** and **Calder Wood**, *076 677*, or *091 698*, 222 acres with riverside woodlands. These Country Parks are well signposted from main roads and are always accessible to walkers.

In Mid Lothian is **Vogrie**, *376 633*, 257 acres of parkland. Vogrie is a new Country Park with oldish estate perimeter woods and very old policy trees, obviously loved as much for their eccentricities as their excellences. The walled garden, now a nursery and garden centre, has a fantastically well-built wall, and not much of the rest comes up to it, but there is a gorgeous unmown patch of grass – with the familiar lowland cocktail of meadowsweet and willow herb – and a grotto-like copse of cherry laurel. Coppiced limes are apparently hybrid but without the usual faults of twiggyness and aphids.

EAST LOTHIAN

John Muir CP, Dunbar *652 788 and 626 810*, ♣, *1668 acres (200 acres woodland), pathless sands, LA*
John Muir was a native of Dunbar who migrated to California aged eleven years. He was one of those far-sighted enough to create one of the first American National Parks, Yosemite, in the same year, 1890, as the National Park of the Giant Forest and the General Grant National Park, now all part of the Sequoia National Park.

Salix alba 'Pendula', Royal Botanic Garden

Vogrie parkland

Pressmennan Wood

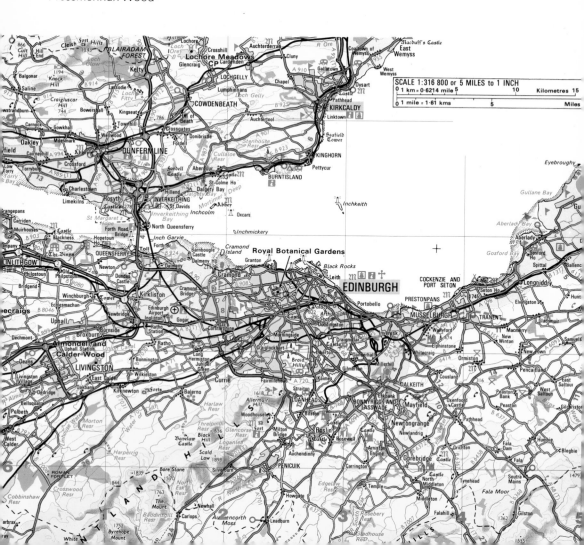

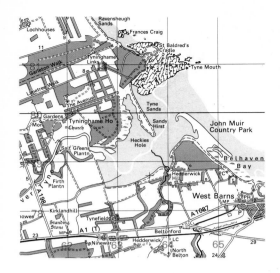

rides streaked with ragwort and vistas stopped by sea buckthorn: fascinating, and a welcome retreat from the sun when I visited. But you will be drawn naturally to the wide shore: pink sand, whitish green grass and miniature forests of sea spurge, leaves as if made of soapy plastic. Maram spikes inscribe circles in the sand. Sea campion, an unlikely heliotrope, adds to a dazzling colour scheme against a sea of inky blue-black.

The large parking place (given first above) is shadeless and has the best designed WCs in Britain, a sawn-off broch shape perfectly suited to the dunes. Scots architecture rarely indulges in half-hearted compromise. The north-east compartment of the park, with more mature pines on the shore, is approached by long, shady lines of Tyninghame Estate trees, via the A198 to North Berwick.

This wide beach with its view of the Bass Rock is a good memorial. There are no *Sequoiadendron*, but you could not expect them in the sand. The pines are a low-profile group,

Pressmennan Wood, Stenton *621 726,*
♀ ♣, *200 acres, 2m walk, FC*
This north-facing slope has wide views reached after a longish slog through a lot of Norway spruce. Oaks near the cark park are supported by guylines, their companion softwoods having been extracted, leaving them

unable to cope with the strong winds. Towards the top of the walk a few oaks remain amongst pines. Descending, never quite to the lake, the path enters dark *Thuja* and *Tsuga* amongst birch and ash, and there are some large beeches and oaks, about 160 years old.

Stenton village is handsome with red tiles, all about is quiet and lovely except for the Forestry Commission car park, which is quiet and dirty. Elms, wych and hybrid, are magnificent by roadsides.

Over the Lammermuir Hills to Whiteadder gives you the same view as from the wood, even broader, with purple heather in the foreground instead of pole conifers. Bees here are transhumed for the heather, transported

In the Lammermuir Hills: Dunbar Common, looking out to Tyne Mouth and the Bass Rock

while they sleep at night by white-clad young ladies in veils. It's true, because I saw it happen!

Whiteadder Water is a last home of native oaks, elms and alders, but most spectacular just below the reservoir, with flat pasture full of multicoloured cattle and dark, forested hills beyond.

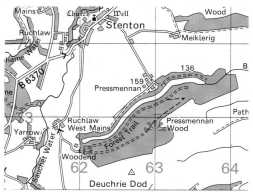

Whiteadder Water

Duns Castle *783 543*, ♀, *3 walks, 2–3m, NR (SWT)*

The town of Duns is supposed to have an oakwood. I could only find the policy woods of the castle, open as a nature reserve, with the lake, agreeably called Hen Poo (Scots for Swan Lake?) and several shady walks. Duns Law, easily accessible from the town, is an ancient fort, 650 feet, patrolled by cows which use the stumps of once massive oaks as rubbing posts. A patch of pines obscures the view of the castle, which is private and much the most impressive thing in the landscape – positively elephantine.

You can enter the estate woods also by a sort of back door from the B6365 at *785 561* (dogs not allowed) and here you do not have to march down carriage drives before reaching the trees.

Hen Poo, Duns Castle

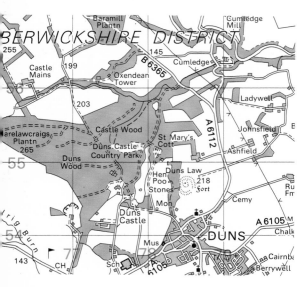

NORTH OF THE FORTH

Lochore Meadows Country Park, *172 962*, is a noble effort to restore 900 acres of pithead to nature, but woodland there is none.

Keen walkers are advised to consider the great circle of the **Lomond Hills**, mountain routes in and out of plantations, clearly illustrated on maps posted at car parks near Falkland. The climb to one of these, East Lomond car park, is 850 feet.

Central Highlands and North Argyll

Landranger sheets 40, 41, 42, 48, 49, 51, 57

RANNOCH

Black Wood of Rannoch *573 565*, ↟,
walks 1 to 5m, forest roads 3m, FC
Of all the woods, the Black Wood of Rannoch
exerts the greatest fascination, through its
name alone. If it were still called the Fir Wood
of Carie it might not sound so romantic; but
even then, glimpses of Rannoch Muir, that
vast, glowering moraine of lochans, rocks and
bogs, put ideas into my head. On discovery,
Loch Rannoch, grey and wild-looking enough
amongst its rather low hills, is just another

loch, albeit protected from the cruder machin-
ations of holiday campers. The wood is on the
south side, and begins not with a deepening of
texture in the moorland as I imagined, but near
a white-painted school. This is, or was, the
House of Dall, and the great pines are here.
Before you reach them the Forestry
Commission attempts to head you off on forest
walks in Allt na Bogair, where its men have
mixed in some more useful, alien species. To
see the pines, ignore all this and park where
you may, about *573 565* – there are two or
three places by the water. A cart track ascends

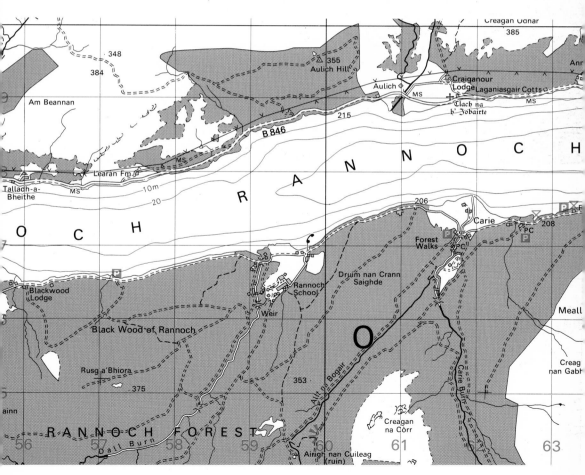

Buttressed trunk of an old pine, Rannoch

into the wood, and then forks east and west. Either track will return you to the lochside, but the western route is shorter and more revealing (keep to the track).

The Forestry Commission took over the Black Wood of Rannoch in 1947, after 8000 trees had been removed during World War II – these were only available because, scheduled for clear felling in 1918, the wood had been saved by the ending of World War I. There was an earlier period of Government ownership in the eighteenth century when the commissioners of forfeited Jacobite estates managed the woodlands carefully, even removing competing birch and alder. Apart

from these two periods of decency, the wood was ill-treated and exploited, only its relative inaccessibility, and the small size of the population it served, preventing its destruction. Floating the timber down the Tummel and the Tay does not *look* as if it could have been easy, and many pines were

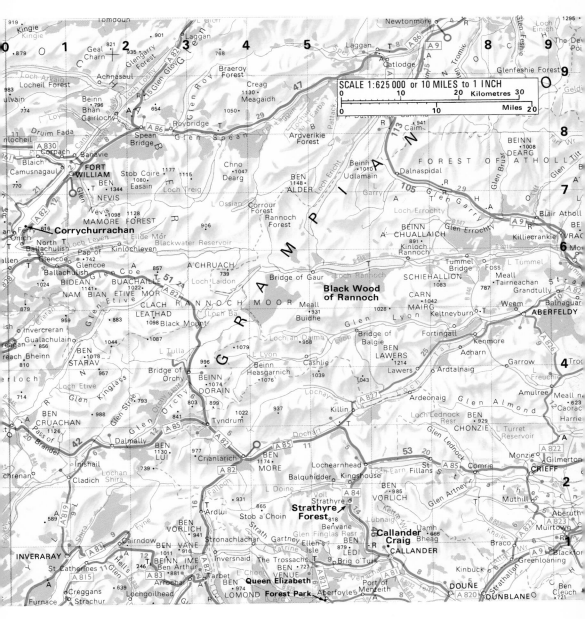

stolen – some were even 'washed up' on the shores of Holland; a nice variant of the back-of-a-lorry story.

Birches accompany the pines, increasing in frequency at the edges. Regeneration, on extraordinarily uneven bog, bilberry and heather, is obviously fine. Several varieties of the native pine are easily picked out: columnar and rounded crowns appear side by side, and there are many other variations of form, the reasons unknown. Great pines about *573 565* are heavily buttressed, and there is also variation in the bark pattern between 'plated' and 'flaky', with old trees very ruggedly ridged

45

Lynn of Tummel

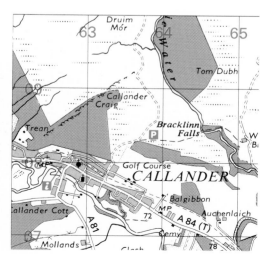

rather like Monterey pines. Juniper is fairly common. It is the variety of form, the curious grouping and the vigour of growth at all stages which give this wood its character – and make it a valuable source of information on genetic and other variations.

To get to Loch Rannoch you have to pass through (or now bypass) the revoltingly touristy main street of Pitlochry, and then you may be waylaid by the Lynn of Tummel, a National Trust for Scotland well-beaten track to a confluence of waters, once a fall, now levelled up by hydroelectric works. At Loch Tummel there is the Queen's View to contend with (and it is a gorgeous loch, among high hills), and then the Forestry Commission's Tummel Forest walks, with slightly less regal views, but with native woodland on limestone rocks. The wetlands between the large lochs are fascinating. Kinloch Rannoch has a garage and three shops, only one of which sells tartan trinkets. Camping is restricted to two sites, one run by the Forestry Commission, class B.

North of Pitlochry the woods of Blair Atholl are famous. They were planted with hardwood trees by the Dukes of Atholl in the eighteenth and nineteenth centuries. The Pass of Killiecrankie contains a woodland nature reserve of 55 acres and there is a much larger RSPB reserve here, with restricted access.

CALLANDER

Callander Craig *636 093*, ♠, *1¼m, steep, FC and LA*
The town is busy, with dozens of tourist attractions, and it is not unusual apparently for a full pipe band to play in a side street. Above the town to the north is Callander Craig, a ridge rising some 650 feet above the town in a matter of yards. You can drive half way up, to a parking ground arranged for the Bracklinn Falls (footpath eastwards) and the Forestry Commission's Callander Craig Walk, which goes off westwards. This way of reaching the craigs is via a very steep climb through some dark spruces – but these are to be opened out for the views, I am told. The other end of the path is signposted on the road 1 mile beyond the car park at *636 093*. You can certainly park

Rannoch Muir

beside the road at several places. The view is worth the climb whichever way you go.

Callander is an entry point for the Queen Elizabeth Forest Park.

Queen Elizabeth Forest Park

The park occupies an area roughly 15 miles by 15, south-west of Callander and bounded by the eastern shore of Loch Lomond. Aberfoyle is the effective centre of the area and the Forestry Commission's David Marshall Lodge, *520 014*, is uphill and north of Aberfoyle. The road from here, lurching and arching northwards to Loch Achray, is the twisting stem to which most of the visitors'

Trossachs mile post, Achray Forest

47

plums are attached. There are several viewpoints, official and unofficial, along the way, not least at the David Marshall Lodge where a landmark-finding plate was presented by the Automobile Association. Inside the Lodge is a pleasant café, a quite superb map and an information desk with the usual range of Forestry Commission material.

From the road northwards, the A821, called the Duke's Pass – our stem – starts a forest drive which takes you on a 7-mile detour by one leg of the quaintly named Loch Drunkie. There are a few oaks here – a narrow strip left undisturbed by the foresters. Otherwise, and unless you are a keen fisherman, this drive is not a well-spent pound. You get a better view for nothing from the viewpoint nearly opposite the drive entrance at *523 046*. At the top of the stem, branching left, is The Trossachs, world famous, but simply an obsolete Gaelic word for a cross-pass. Here a formidable symmetry of granite welcomes visitors to a large car park, not costly, and an array of facilities designed to extract a certain amount of cash. The best

value is almost certainly the charming steamboat which leaves at 11 o'clock in the morning for a voyage on Loch Katrine, calling at Stronachlachar at about 11.40. I missed the boat.

The Achray Forest, each side of the Duke's Pass, is thoroughly planted with spruces and looks quite magnificent from any angle. The foreground is often comparatively empty – bracken and heather studded with native birches, and a perfect foil to the richly shaped and wooded hills. Don't be put off by the somewhat touristy atmosphere; it's all lovely, and the planting is entirely appropriate to the country.

There are fourteen different woodland walks as well as a wayfaring course, and 70 miles of waymarked long walks through the forest, with coloured chevrons: yellow for Aberfoyle, black for Callander, green for Brig o' Turk (Trossachs), and so on. Several of the walks are orientated to east Loch Lomondside in our Section 64.

The Trossachs tree may be said to be rooted

The view south-west from the David Marshall Lodge, Queen Elizabeth Forest Park

in the mysterious, roadless, Flanders Moss, where the youthful Forth meanders. At the northern edge of the Moss, the Lake of Menteith with the island Priory of Inchmahome has a nature reserve of 110 acres. On Flanders Moss the tall birches were once burnt with the heather so that invaders from the south (from the Roman army onwards) could not advance in concealment. The Highlands here supported a fairly high population. The people herded deer for slaughter and sometimes raided the Lowland cattle, and in general probably built up an exaggerated reputation for outrageous behaviour, as for instance was attached to Robin Oig of the MacGregor clan. The rather complex history of the region is explained by A. S. MacNaire in the Forestry Commission guide. Contributors deal with geology, botany, birds and animals, freshwater biology, forestry and walks, to which H. E. Edlin, that great writer on trees, adds a note on 'The Trossachs and Literature', irresistibly quoting the 'Solitary Reaper' of Wordsworth:

Will no-one tell me what she sings?
Perhaps the plaintive numbers flow
For old unhappy far-off things,
And battles long ago . . .

Strathyre Forest, by Loch Lubnaig, north-west of Callander, has a nature trail at *560 168* and a walk to the Falls of Leny at *595 090*. The Information Centre is in Strathyre village. Facilities offered in this forest include some tougher walks.

FORT WILLIAM

South of Fort William, there is a useful picnic place at Corrychurrachan, *045 662*; turn off the A82(T) 1½ miles north of the Corran Ferry. Or, after the excitement of Glencoe, turn right in Glencoe village for Kinlochleven. There are several stopping places around the lake, with small streams and an abundance of rowan. North-bound traffic uses the bridge at Ballachulish; if you do not want the detour around Loch Leven you can instead turn right

Flanders Moss

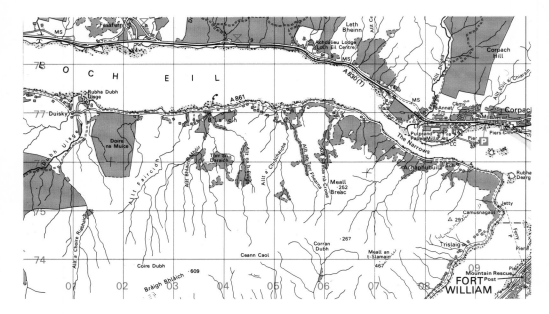

Loch Eil

at Inchree, 1 mile north of Onich, for a picnic place and a short walk to the waterfall.

The ferry at Corran provides a short-cut to Glen Tarbert and Sunart, and to Mull, and quite incidentally has preserved the A861 along the south shore of Loch Eil in a condition of amazing grace. Fort William is a patch of irritant to be got through by travellers to the Western Highlands, and one forgets that its setting is so spectacular – under Ben Nevis – yet on the shores of a sea loch.

A861, **Loch Eil** 965 787 to 095 765, ♀, *6m of lochside road*

Loch Eil is gently tidal, and the mossy oaks which line her southern shores have the true character of the rural Highlands, untouched by twentieth-century engineering and chemistry. There are patches of extremely rich vegetation and dozens of places to stop and enjoy the views across the water; fantastic on a misty, sunny August morning. Traffic is purely local; farming and fishing.

MORVERN, SUNART, MULL

At Lochaline I looked rather longingly at the ferry to Mull as it steamed in the silver Sound,

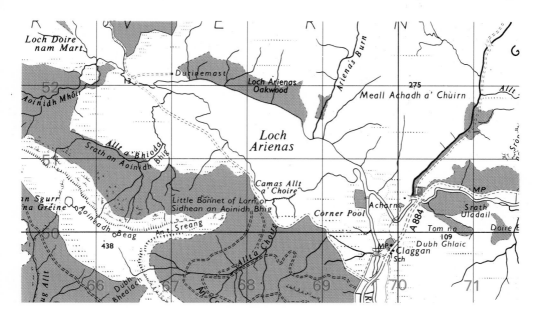

The Sound of Mull from Lochaline

but, behind schedule, I had to stay on the mainland. The reason for the journey westward is a lochside oakwood.

Loch Arienas Oakwood *672 523*, ♀, *150 acres, NR*
The wood is part of the large Rahoy Hills nature reserve of 4325 acres. Recommended access is by Acharn, *701 505*, about a mile south-east of the wood, where you can park in the patchy shade of fine oak trees. A good track leads up to the Black Glen (Gleann Dubh) north-eastwards where, also, there are small native oakwoods. The quickest way to the

Durinemast, Loch Arienas

Loch Arienas oaks

Fiunary Forest spruces

lochside wood is to take the minor road signed to Kinloch, parking by the turn-off to Durinemast Cottage. There is a sort of path above the cottage. Remarkably wind-cut at the edges, the trees within are normal durmast oaks (though the leaves have rather short stalks and are slightly eared), and with the oaks grow rowan, wych elm and ash.

Here you can be really 'away from it all'. Even so, you cannot get away from the Forestry Commission. On the mountainside south of Loch Arienas the tall spruces of the Fiunary Forest are planted like corn through which giant swathes are cut as the trees are harvested.

Other oakwoods rather closer to Fort William are at Strontian (A861): turn north to Ariundle, then signposted, *831 638*. A nature trail leads through the woods to old lead mines. There is a woodland car park also west of Strontian, at *745 620*, with a walk on the cliff above Loch Sunart.

MULL

On the island I must leave you in the hands of the Forestry Commission with, by Tobermory, the Ardmore Forest Walk, *485 557*, reached by the Glengorm Castle road, $\frac{1}{2}$ mile west of the town. South-east of Craignure, *721 369*, is a cliff path to Torosay Castle.

Tayside and Deeside

Landranger sheets 43, 44, 45, 53, 54, 58, 59

Tentsmuir Forest *500 242*
Comparatively easily reached from Edinburgh, the enormous, flat Tentsmuir pine forest on the sands north of St Andrews has a Forestry Commission picnic place on Kinshaldy Beach.

Edensmuir, Ladybank *292 095*, ♠,
2 short walks, FC
Situated east of the Lomond Hills, this is a really lovely pine plantation, balanced between the extremes of hill and beach. In mature open woodland the children can be adventurous, while remaining visible. One tired-looking man had pitched a tent and settled down to doze. Another, probably tired-looking, wrote copy and drank coffee, while little Scottish girls in Sunday flounces set off on walks. Such domestic touches apart, it is hard to say just why this pinewood on flat land is so attractive: age perhaps contributes most.

PERTH

Kinnoull Hill Woods and **Deuchny Wood** *135 235 and 145 236*, ♀ ♠, *various routes, NR, FC*
The Kinnoull nature reserve on the Rhine-style crags above the Tay at Perth is nicely appointed and easily accessible. A well-worn path leads steeply into birch and oakwood. The trail connects with the Forestry Commission's Deuchny Wood and Kinfauns Jubilee Walk, which cheats a bit by following the contours for a mile or so out of the woods: but the view is marvellous. Pines and spruces of Deuchny are varied by a beech plantation, the bark here being sage green spotted with the greys of lichen. Approach by Kinfauns village off the A85(T) to Dundee, if you are not in Perth. If you are, take a bus to Kinnoull Hill or look out for signs on Dundee Road. Do not walk

Edensmuir

there through the streets, it is too steep and exhausting.

Also well signposted off Dundee Road, Perth, is Branklyn, a world famous National Trust for Scotland garden of 2 acres with tree magnolias and other fine garden trees, open March to October.

Scone Palace *114 266*, ♀ ♣ (♣), *Arboretum, 40 acres, pf*
The palace is visited by thousands eager to see the gold of the Scottish kings; the park entrance is off the road – the A93 to Glen Blairgowrie – in Old Scone. Turn left for the arboretum, which has an original Douglas fir

from seed sent home by the explorer to his father, who was head gardener here. A most impressive assemblage of silver firs, *Sequoiadendron* and Sitka spruce were planted in a simple grid in 1860, around some earlier specimens. When I was there *Sciadopitys*, rare in the north, was in cone – each and every one out of reach of the camera in a poor light.

As I left this conifer cathedral to walk towards the palace the late sun flashed from under the cloud, making a white poplar by the terrace gleam – as if with the silver of the Scottish arboriculturalists.

DUNKELD

A complex of woodlands and tree places is centred on the little town, which, on a Sunday in July, was not too crowded for comfort. Tay salmon in a pub was reasonably priced and the accents in the bar were local. By the half-ruined cathedral stand the mothers of all Scottish larches, so it is said, very tall and elegant on the lawn beside the river. Some, 130 feet high, were planted in 1750. Here, on the estate of the Dukes of Atholl, emerged the hybrid between this European larch and the Japanese, called the Dunkeld larch, which has proved more productive and disease-resistant in Britain than its parents.

Deuchny Wood above Perth

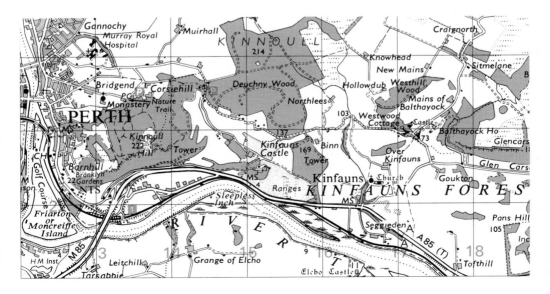

The Dukes of Atholl were leaders in the late eighteenth century in planting over 10,000 acres of previously unproductive moorland, much of it with larch.

From Dunkeld north-west to Pitlochry, the Atholl area contains twelve sites of natural-history interest, but in summer it also contains a lot of people.

Hermitage Woods *012 423*, ✦
(off A9[T]), 1½m, riverside, NTS
The 8th Duke intended this tree garden, first planted in the eighteenth century, to come to the Trust, of which he was the first president. All the specimen trees are gone and *Pseudotsuga menziesii* is the present dominant, as we are informed by the National Trust and the Forestry Commission with notices in different styles on each side of the water. The centre-piece is the Black Linn, by the folly called Ossian's Hall (which originally was a hall of mirrors, not enjoyed by Wordsworth). Ossian was a somewhat mythical, if not

actually false, third-century Gaelic bard.

The pool is fantastically marbled with foam from the churning falls, and well worth a trip through the sweet wrappers. The more masculine, resinous Forestry Commission trail can be joined here. I followed the glen to look for native oaks, and found a few with mossy bases amongst hard fern, not enough to alter the falsity of this coniferized honeypot. How can it be restored now, either to the arboretum intended or to the oakwood it should naturally be? A problem.

Loch of Lowes, *041 435*, is a nature reserve with long woodland walks around the loch, and on the ridge of Craig Wood, once coppiced: probably a better choice than the Hermitage. Instead I went to look at the **Meikleour Beech Hedge**, *163 385*, a legendary row of beeches 650 yards long and 90 feet high. It isn't much of a walk, being along the A93, but is a very effective screen for Meikleour House which sets the tone, in the long, wide valley of

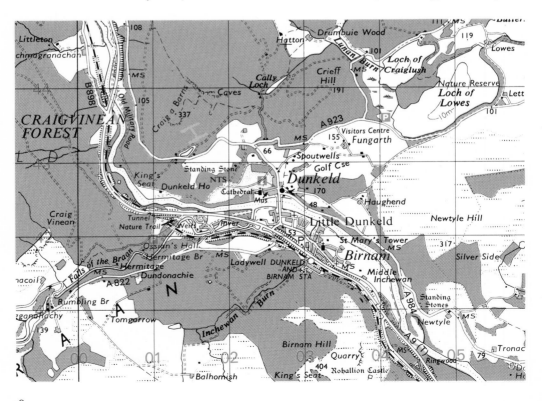

Strathmore, for a high standard of tree planting, patterning the placid, clear-cut landscape that is more like central Ireland than anything left in England.

Eastwards, **Glamis Castle**, blushing and demure amongst her policy *Pseudotsugas*, has magnificent trees all around, with very Scottish effects, like copper beeches placed next to white poplars, whose leaves show their silver backs in the perpetual breezes. The castle, a mile away from the village at *385 481*, is approachable any afternoon in summer except on Saturdays. Out of hours the road, the A928, is quieter than any Surrey lane.

Montreathmont Forest *557 531*, ♣, *3000 acres, no walks, FC*

The name Montreath further emphasizes the similarity with the centre of Ireland. The vast and romantic-looking forest, mainly of pine, inhabits what must have been a frightening expanse of wet heathland. If it is peace and quiet you seek, come here. I have spent the day writing and have seen no one, except when I went to get some milk. About ten cars may have passed, and one four-engined aeroplane – and that almost silently, freewheeling into Dundee for breakfast. Nothing grows on the forest floor except three or four species of fern, some mosses and a grey, inedible-looking *Boletus*. The scenery changes imperceptibly

Eyebright, Montreathmont

Black Linn, Hermitage Woods

from the deep dusk of Sitka to the less deep dusk of Norway spruce, brightening slightly in the Scots pine. A road runs through the middle for 2 miles, straight as a spruce. There are plenty of places to stop; only one if you want actually to park and write your book. This is near Red Roofs, by Guthrie. Mr and Mrs McKay (pronounced Key) do bed and beakfast. The parking place is full of a hairy-stemmed eyebright, as pretty a minute flower as you can imagine: delicately pleated, white, frilly-edged petals, a patch of clear yellow and lines of black finer than any eyelash. The leaves are half folded and triangular, ruggedly serrated. And each one of the thousands of these quarter-inch flowers is perfect.

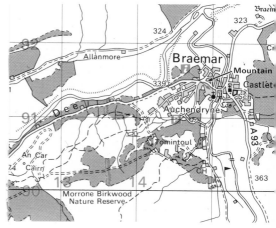

The bird cherry is not well known in the British countryside, but it is our only native *Prunus* to have a fossil record before Roman times. It can be found in northern and eastern England but is common by streams in parts of the Highlands. The blossom, in splendid spires, appears in June on Speyside, reflecting the mountain snows.

LEFT: Montreathmont Forest

BRAEMAR AND LINN OF DEE

Braemar: Morrone Birkwood *143 911*, ♀, *560 acres, NNR*
Every glen has its birches, not so much in Scotland the 'Lady of the Woods' as a gaggle of village girls, all shapes and sizes. But at Braemar, on the slopes of Morrone, 2819 feet, is a gathering of really lovely birches, in most lights making a delicate pattern of greys on the uneven ground. These woods are of pure, downy birch with juniper, rich in lichens, biophytes and ferns. There are similar woods in Norway, but visitors from Scandinavia might be surprised at the irregularity of the Scottish trees.

Betula pubescens, Braemar

61

Meanders of the Dee above Braemar: rain storm approaching

You are expected to keep to the footpaths. There is a viewpoint at Tomintoul and a parking place at Auchendryne, at the map reference, or you can walk up from the town quite easily. There are views over the wide flood plain of the Dee and the Cairngorm mountains beyond.

Linn of Dee to Linn of Quoich *065 898*, ✦, *5–6m, pf*

There are fine stands of spruce as well as pine in the Dee glen, but the remains of the Forest of Mar are in the glens of Derry and Quoich (as well as in the royal estate of Ballochbuie) and it needs some determination to reach them. However, there are scattered old trees on the hillside north-west of the Linn of Dee, and a relatively easy walk up to Glen Lui and then north-east across to Glen Quoich can give one a fair cross-section of the vegetation. This is a walk of 5 or 6 miles however, depending on what short-cuts you can make (see the map on the next page). Topographically it is fairly simple since you are only going up one glen, crossing a short stretch of moor and then coming down the next glen. There is a fine planted pinewood on the hillside west of the Linn of Quoich.

For two centuries there has been a heavy red deer population and consequently little regeneration. Timber was extracted from the whole of the Forest of Mar in the eighteenth century, but the difficulty of transport has

Scots pines in the Mar Forest

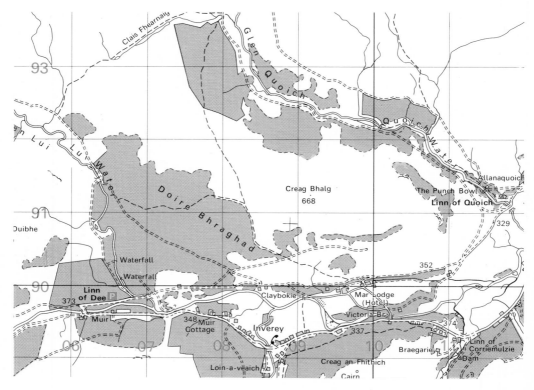

Middle Deeside country

Trees regenerate on the Muir of Dinnet

protected the upper glens, while Queen Victoria personally protected the trees of Ballochbuie. Logs were floated down the Dee, but only on flood water, so that bridges were frequently destroyed. The writer Pennant in 1769 visited Ouvercauld and described a 'magnificent forest of pines many miles in extent'. The sawmill regularly produced planks 10 feet long, 11 inches wide and 3 inches thick. These were sold for two shillings each, which does not sound much but was more than a labourer's weekly wage. There are records of many whole Scots pines being sold for sixpence each.

Muir of Dinnet *431 997 (Burn o' Vat)*, ♀ ♠ ♨, *3600 acres, NNR*

This magnificent stretch of country includes lochs at Davan and Kinord, and according to the legend on the notice-board map 'land formed by glacial meltwater including kettle lochs, dry channels, unique pot holes (the Vat) and a complex of sand and gravel deposits'. The heather and bearberry moor shows a strong tendency to return to forest, with birch and pine spreading rapidly and offering 'a challenge to conservation'. I hope that challenge will be met by supineness, so that a natural forest may be formed. Older woodland is at New Kinord.

I have for once given a parking place reference which I did not visit: I entered the reserve from the A93. The reserve is cut by the A97, south to north, but you are not conscious of this in the view eastwards, which is absolutely splendid in the evening sun (and no doubt in other lights as well). Pines over purple heather at the edge of the reserve are no doubt the results of careful husbandry, effective nonetheless. Lady's mantle grows amongst the heather. This is a nature reserve which is sure to repay study and while not of primary

Lady's mantle, Dinnet

woodland is, as it were, pregnant with woodland. There is a great variety and richness of habitat with large numbers of insect species and seventy-six breeding bird species.

The beautiful Dinnet oakwood, *464 980*, is south of the town. It is a National Nature Reserve of 30 acres containing both sessile and pedunculate oaks and their hybrid.

Glen Tanar contains a fine native Scots pine wood with juniper, rowan, aspen and birch – a National Nature Reserve. There is a Visitors' Centre at Braeloine. The NCC's map reference is No 4891.

Crathes Castle *734 968*, ♀ ♣, *600 acres, NTS*

Not at all remote, wild or forbidding, this is an astonishingly rich and tree-saturated place. In summer it could be described as visitor-saturated too, but out of season you will not be charged to park (you can always make a small donation). Escaping the crowds, I found many unusual trees by the entrance lodge. There is a beautiful lake, also surrounded by trees. The lawns, gardens and ancient hedges by the castle are impressive and very carefully and exploitively planted. Even an old quarry at the edge of the estate contains pretty birches and bird cherries. There are waymarked walks, with a leaflet. There is a resident ranger naturalist, Mr Karl Pipes (Crathes 651).

The whole of Middle Deeside, with seventeen sites of special interest to naturalists, is both a nature reserve and an established tourist attraction – the two are still compatible in Scotland. Oakwoods at Craigendarroch and Aboyne, at Dinnet and Drum, are of varied interest – old coppices at Craigendarroch. Pines are spreading over the moors of the Glen Tanar estate and in parts of the Ballochbuie Forest, which have been fenced. Birch is the dominant tree, but native cherries of both species reveal themselves in early summer. The waters of the Dee are pure. Farming is not a major preoccupation.

Crathes Castle; a Camperdown elm

Western Highlands and Glen More Forest
Landranger sheets 19, 23, 24, 26, 27, 32, 33, 36

70	
68	69
66	67

LOCH MAREE

In a survey commissioned by the National Trust for Scotland, 56 areas of natural beauty were selected, only 13 of which it was decided had not been spoiled in some way. Of these 13, the Torridon area, including Loch Maree, came high on the list. It is good to be critical, but the Trust must surely be mistaken in limiting its area of influence. In concentrating on certain 'perfect' areas it has attracted too many visitors to those sites. All of the Scottish Highlands, and most of the Lowlands, are beautiful; all should have been declared a National Park long ago. The Scottish National Scenic Areas, the equivalent of the English Areas of Outstanding Natural Beauty, do not seem to be well known. The authorities responsible for the Scottish countryside should spend money first and foremost on clearing away wires, and it should get the money from taxing touring caravans as they cross the border. At present the only gainers are Kodak and the garages.

Scotland *is* a separate problem in terms of conservation, and this is recognized; but the problem has not yet been properly stated, and solutions will not be found by a cautious and selective approach. Only the Forestry Commission with its wide spread of thoroughly implemented public-access programmes has had any significant effect; but the Forestry Commission is primarily interested in timber production and is bound to compromise.

Loch Maree, with its surrounding shining mountains, is, in a sense, indestructible. Yet already the process of destruction-by-visitor has begun. The road, which used to be a Highland road, a single track of tarmacadam carefully picking its way from rock to rock, is

Loch Maree

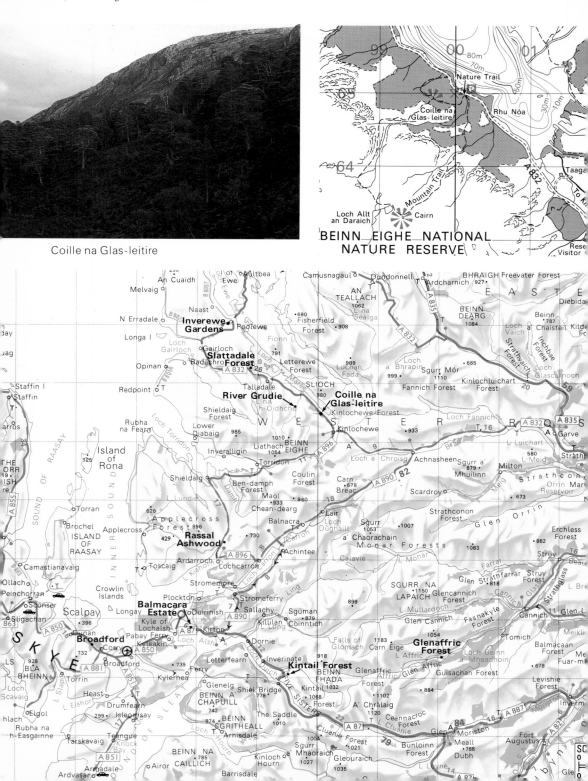

Coille na Glas-leitire

now typically a well-engineered and finely surfaced one with neat, white curbs: destruction of wildness by framing the scene. Kinlochewe is virtually nothing but a tourist town. The Beinn Eighe National Nature Reserve, containing the natural stand of pines in Coille na Glas-leitire, has a Visitors' Centre and is somehow thus reduced to a museum exhibit. Once you are out of the way of these necessary facilities, nature reasserts herself.

But before all this, the hydroelectric wires pioneered their own route across what is now the nature reserve, and there they remain. You can avoid them, but I am quite certain they should have been buried long ago.

Coille na Glas-leitire 002 650, ♣ (Scots pines), nature trails, short, medium or long, NNR

The Beinn Eighe National Nature Reserve is the oldest in Britain, 10,500 acres established in 1951. The woods cover about 500 acres and the nature trails start from the parking place at the reference above. You pass the Visitors' Centre on your way from Kinlochewe. The dignified shapes of the pines, surprisingly green and soft looking, are scattered up the sides of the 'Combe of the Steep Hillside'. Avoid late summer evenings – midges are fierce.

Slattadale Forest 888 723, ♣ (Norway spruce), 1000 acres, 3 forest walks, FC

There is an island in this most beautiful of lochs: on that island a lochan, and in the lochan an islet. On the islet once grew a great pine. Surely the centre of the world! Not surprisingly the fairies gathered here, and the island, Subhainn, with its neighbour islands, seems to float with a cargo of trees: no doubt there are boat trips from the Loch Maree Hotel, where Queen Victoria once stayed.

The Forestry Commission is cutting down its spruces, and a strong smell of diesel oil rises from the settlement by the shore. The walks are: 5 miles to Poolewe, 1 mile in the trees, and a short path to see the falls named after Victoria. The Forestry Commission calls the forest Achnashellach, and this includes,

Slattadale, Loch Maree

besides Slattadale, the much softer sounding, and very large, Flowerdale Forest, where flowers are few and trees are absent. But, as mist rose in a cloud from the high Loch Badan Sgalaig, revealing a perfect inverted mountain amongst the dew-encrusted reeds, I forgot, for a while, about trees and woods.

Struggling alder in the River Grudie

Inverewe

River Grudie *966 678, ♀ ♣, about 3m, fp, NR*

It seems a century since, researching my first tree book, I plodded up the little river to see what native trees grew in this remote but basically benign environment. A small island where the stream divides and animals are discouraged is crowded with pines and other trees. Holly, alder and rowan struggle in the banks where the champing jaws cannot quite reach – but the waters can. Somehow the little trees survive the floods. In places where the banks of peat are cut away by the water are enormous whitened roots of forgotten pines and even oaks.

There are stands of pines and a beautiful wood of birch where the river flows into the loch. Up the river appear the sculptured peaks of Beinn Eighe. In all this rocky splendour, the search for woodlands seems somewhat irrelevant. But it would be nice to see a fenced-off area for natural regeneration near the river.

Inverewe Gardens, Poolewe *864 819, ♀ ♣, NTS*

Over a century ago Osgood MacKenzie found only one tree, a dwarf willow, on his peaty headland. He made a deer and rabbit fence and planted a thick belt of Scots pine and Corsican pine, then hedges of *Rhododendron ponticum* which sheltered native trees, and larch and Douglas fir. Silver firs, *Tsuga, Thuja, Cupressus* and *Chamaecyparis* followed, and even *Sequoiadendron* where there was sufficient depth for the roots. Soil was brought in by the creel, seaweed used for fertilizer. Now there are tall woodlands for the walks and to shelter exotic plants. In the section called Bamboozelem are the Bamboo *Arundinaria murieli* and many unusual trees including a large *Magnolia campbellii, Dicksonia* tree ferns, several *Eucalyptus, Myrtus, Sciadopitys,* a *Drimys aromatica*. There is *Drimys winteri* elsewhere. This tree, Winter's bark, was discovered in South America by one of Francis Drake's captains as a much-needed cure for scurvy. Giant rhododendrons are a feature of the garden, as at the Savill Gardens in Windsor Park. Everywhere are blue hydrangeas. 'When is the best time to visit Inverewe?' is the

Rassal Ashwood, in the part not fenced

subject of a page in the booklet, which has a good foreword by MacKenzie's daughter.
I would say the best time is in May, which has the lowest rainfall, next to the highest hours of sun and is too early for blue hydrangeas.

There are nearly 2000 acres of land at Inverewe, although most of the action is in a tenth of this. Nearly 100,000 visitors a year pay approximately a pound a head. The Trust runs an international-standard campsite nearby, bookable (Poolewe 249). The post office at Poolewe sells exotic and unusual cheeses amongst a wide range of ordinary groceries.

The National Trust for Scotland's country-side of Torridon, centre at *905 557*, is not particularly noted for its trees; more for its geology, scenery and wildlife. However, native pines can be seen by Loch Torridon. The history of the Trust property of 16,000 acres is interesting. Most, 14,000 acres, was accepted in *part* payment of death duties after the demise of the 4th Earl of Lovelace; then transferred to the Trust through 'national land fund procedures'. The ranger naturalist is Mr Lea MacNally (Torridon 221).

SOUTHWARDS

Rassal Ashwood *843 433*, ♀, *200 acres, NNR*

On a lumpy limestone platform covered by bright green moss are the lovely white and green trunks of the most northerly ashwood in Britain. There are also sallows and hazels which, fallen or riven by storms, put up their own strong coppice shoots. Part is fenced, and the richness of grass and herbs has to be seen to be believed, with moorland desert all around. Wild strawberries at this latitude? See for yourself, but go carefully, both to protect the woodland and your own ankles.

These are 200 acres of truth amongst millions under the rule of the Highland sheep. Of course, there are not many limestone outcrops. Nevertheless, the vegetation of the Highlands could be fantastically rich compared to what it is.

Kyle of Lochalsh: Balmacara Estate
798 276, woodland garden, NTS
The National Trust for Scotland owns most of the Lochalsh Peninsula, 5600 acres, largely

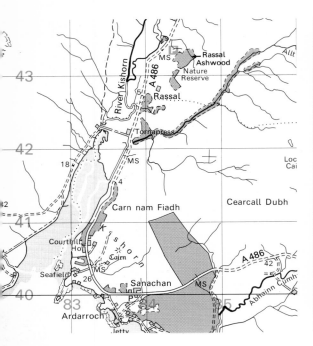

Dwarf oaks, Sleat peninsula, Skye

bare rock and heather, and has attempted to concentrate interest in a waterside plantation, with a natural history display in the coach house of Lochalsh House (which itself is not open). To the north over the headland is Plockton, said to be photogenic. East in the loch is the certainly photogenic Eilean Donnan Castle. **Kintail Forest**, 12,800 acres, without many trees, is also National Trust land, with a centre at Morvich, *961 211*, in the crook of the road by Loch Duich. The A87(T) is now short-circuited, avoiding Morvich.

SKYE

From Kyle the ferry leaves every few minutes for Kyleakin and Skye. No one seriously goes to Skye for woodland walks, which might seem irrelevant in this remarkable place, at least until one has admired its astonishing mountains and learnt something of its crofting history. See Francis Thompson's *The Highlands and Islands*, 1974, for a good, biased summary. He remarks about the one-eighth of the island's 672 square miles which is now forested, that while Sitka spruce is well suited

to the climate, so are hill sheep and cattle. 'More co-operation between farming and forestry interests would create a better environment and programme of land use. Forestry could provide, in belts of trees, shelter for stock, something which most of Skye lacks.' He wonders if the Forestry Commission's drainage techniques (and capital) could not be used to improve the pasture for cattle.

So, my sweeping remarks about the Highland desert cannot be applied to an island community which has struggled so long for its living and its rights in the land. Reduced from 23,000 people in 1841 to 6500 today, whether it likes it or not (everyone is very civil!) the island is host to 500,000 or more tourists a year. Further comment, by a day tripper like me, can hardly clarify the picture. I did see some old hazel coppice, and some scrub oak on the cliffs, in the Sleat peninsula, where I also saw some very unproductive-looking moors. In Sleat is Armadale Castle, *638 049*, ancient home of the Lords of the Isles and the Clan Donald. The clan now owns 17,000 acres for all Macdonalds, and you can join too – it is a charitable trust. At Armadale there is a nature trail and the policy trees are in effect an arboretum. Conifer plantations above give shelter but were devastated in the gale of January 1984, as were some of the estate beeches. The Trail leaflet is nicely set out and includes a good drawing of the early nineteenth-century farm buildings (point 14 on the trail). Point 12 reveals alder and birch woodlands; at point 6 we are invited to 'Have a rest beneath the honeysuckle'. . . . On the moors 1200 black-faced sheep graze 6000 acres.

In the west of the island is Dunvegan Castle, *246 491*, ancient home of the Macleods and once accessible only by sea, they say. The nursery produces tons of vegetables and flowers and the woods of the castle policies to the east of the castle, planted in the late eighteenth century, are open to walkers – an environment in extreme contrast with most of the island's landscape. In between these two oases the Forestry Commission has a picnic place at *425 260* in the Glen Brittle Forest: views of the Cuillin Hills. Walks start from points on the A850 south of Portree and the A855, 7 miles north of Portree. Another walk is from a small car park at *625 249*, 1½ miles west of Broadford (or about 8 miles from Kyleakin).

Ferries are seven days a week from Kyle, six days from Mallaig, summer only from Glenelg.

INVERNESS

Five miles east is Culloden Muir, site of the battle in 1746. A road was built over the 54-foot-long grave of the Mackintosh clan in 1835, but in 1881 the 10th Laird of Culloden built a fine cairn and marked the graves. He had preserved the farmhouse of Old Leanach, heather thatched. The battle, when a thousand weary, hungry Highlanders were destroyed in one hour, marked the end of the Jacobite rebellion – and hastened the 'destruction of a social and economic order' to use the words of the *National Trust for Scotland Guide*. The National Trust for Scotland took over in 1944 from the 13th Laird and the Highland Society of Inverness, and managed in 1972 to demolish a bungalow, built in 1937 on the site. What has all this to do with woodland walks? Well, the

Forestry Commission's **Culloden Forest** covers most of the battlefield. There is a trail called the Forestry Commission Battlefield Trail, *718 456*.

The Forestry Commission also has, 1½ miles north-east of Inverness, near Smithton, a *jogging track* in Douglas fir woodland, with seven exercise stations!

Torrachilty Forest *452 574*, ⚑, *4 forest walks, FC*

There are beautiful Lawson cypresses along the road, the A832, as it rises from Loch Garve, north-west of Inverness, into the richly forested Glen of the Black Water. By Contin is a large picnic place deep in the larchwoods: a trail and a short walk lead into birchwoods. There is a system of paths around the Rogie Falls, *443 586*. A picnic place at the little Loch Achilty, *426 564*, is also in birchwoods.

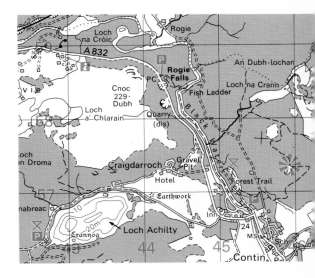

Ardross Forest
Visible from viewpoints official and unofficial on the 'short-cut' road, the A836, from the A9(T) at Evanton to Bonar Bridge, are thousands of acres of steep mountainside scored with the massive trenches through the peat which make it possible to plant trees. This is landscape design on the grand scale. No one can fail to be impressed, provided the weather allows one to see it at all.

Black Isle

The Information Centre at Muir of Ord, Ross and Cromarty Region, provides a booklet, *Walks on the Black Isle*, which lists nineteen walks. I'm afraid I did not visit this peninsula, but it looked attractive and sunny, escaping the mountain weather.

Nairn

A detour through Ardersier from the A96 onto the B9092 will bring you to a drive-in pine forest, *805 550*; very attractive though surrounded by industrial and danger areas. It could be a useful place to stop, with wide grassy verges full of wild flowers.

Turn to Section 69 for the Culbin Forest.

GLEN AFFRIC

The more attractive route to Glen Affric is by Beauly to Cannich – there is a picnic spot at *469 427* – or you can follow the side of Loch Ness from Inverness as far as Drumnadrochit. From Cannich there is only one road apart from a possible left turn at Fasnakyle Power Station.

Very beautiful birch woodland fills the glen by the road, above and below the Dog Falls, where there is a popular parking place at *286 284* and a forest walk through birch and pine. The birches show an extraordinary variety of form from tall to squat and bushy.

The woodlands by Loch Affric and Loch Beinn a' Mheadhoin are important native pinewoods. This was a timber-producing area flourishing in the eighteenth century, logs being floated down the Rivers Cannich, Glass and Beauly, with a large sawmill at Kilmorack Falls on the Beauly. Then sheep, fire and deer preservation further reduced the forest by limiting natural regeneration.

There were some young trees among the more sheltered heather (ling) when the Forestry Commission took over in 1951. But the foresters found it necessary to fence in the native forest and kill all the deer they could, irrespective of age or sex. They have planted pines from native seed in a 'natural' manner.

A drive-in forest near Nairn

I think they overdid it. As you approach from the final car park at the head of Loch Beinn a' Mheadhoin you are confronted by a neat notice announcing 'The Native Pines of Glen Affric'. All sense of wildness and all sense of discovery are lost: but great beauties remain.

Glenaffric Forest

From the last car park, *201 234*, at the head of Loch Beinn a' Mheadhoin is a very short circuit round a section of old pinewood.
To explore the forest, cross the bridge, whence you will reach a fork in the forest road and the notice mentioned above.

Going left takes you along the shore of Loch Beinn a' Mheadhoin and is not particularly enlightening. The loch was raised 20 feet by the Scottish hydroelectric authority and it may be this which gives it a Mediterranean look, especially in the brilliant sunlight which prevailed over most of my Scottish tours. I expected to find a path branching off uphill to join the forest road at a higher level, but was disappointed and had to trudge back along the

Birches at Dog Fall

Glen Affric pines. OVERLEAF: Loch Beinn a' Mheadhoin

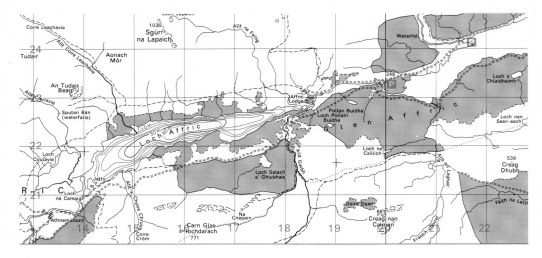

hot, stony road. More of the same is one's lot if
one turns right at the fork and up the glen.
A small detour brings the relief of a lochan
with white water-lilies, surrounded by white,
dead trees; otherwise more stony road. A
complete circuit of Loch Affric involves you in
a 10-mile hike – not too much for the beauty of
the place, but you need all day. The footpath
on the north side of the glen gives views of the
forest and the lochs, but is not in woodland.
Glen Affric Lodge, with its footbridge, is
private; you can go across the bridge, but the
dogs will howl at you. In spite of various
difficulties, accentuated by gruelling heat,
surely not a common hazard, Glen Affric and
Loch Beinn a' Mheadhoin are very beautiful
and should not be missed. Indeed, to see the
pines before they are overtaken by the Forestry
Commission's panic planting, go soon. Most of
the old trees are of rounded habit, with bark
pattern plated rather than scaly.

SPEYSIDE: AVIEMORE

Stylish and modern, Aviemore is an
international skiing and leisure centre. It has
its own nature reserve, at Craigellachie, *882
124*, but for the Glen More Forest Park, cross
the Spey and drive about 6 miles to the east
side of Loch Morlich. Just by the large
campsite is the Information Centre where a
leaflet about the forest trails is supposed to be

always available. There are now car parks by
the sandy shores of Loch Morlich, a beautiful
lake 1000 feet above sea-level with trees and
mountains all around.

The Cairngorms National Nature Reserve is
the largest in Britain, 64,220 acres (Visitors'
Centre near Loch Morlich, *978 098*). The
reserve is a mountain area. Only 4000 acres are
forested, but part of this is the small
Rothiemurchus Forest, well known as a
remnant of the original Caledonian pine forest.
The Queen's Forest, by Loch Morlich, is a
forestry plantation, much of which was burnt
down about 1970. Between the two is an
intermediate area of trees, half natural, half
planted.

Glen More Forest Park *977 098*, ♠ ♀
*(pine and birch), 4000 acres, many paths,
FC*

The immediate area of the campsite is
thoroughly explored by footpaths. Take the
Pinewood Trail, $1\frac{1}{4}$ miles, for a glimpse of the
old forest.

My walk took all day and was calculated to
explore the whole range of vegetation. I
followed convenient paths southwards and
then westwards, around Loch Morlich but in
the trees. Taking routes which tended uphill I
reached the tree-line near the small summit of
Castle Hill. The whole Spey Valley can be seen
from here, with its distinctive pattern of light

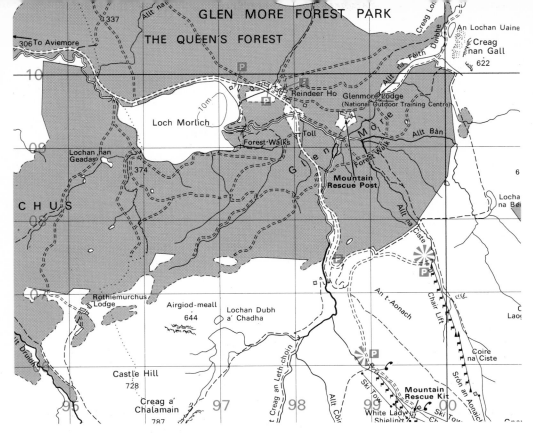

Dwarf birch is woody and deciduous but described as herbaceous because it does not even reach the stature of a shrub. Such miniature 'trees' are adapted to tundra or to windswept, cold heaths. They demand full light and are not woodland plants, but *Betula nana* may form dwarf woods, bitten from above by the deer and no taller than the surrounding heather. The picture was taken within sight of the Cairngorms.

and dark green; birch and pine. I then struck across the moor in a generally south-easterly direction to meet a mountain footpath at 965 055. The trail home was easy walking with tremendous views of the forest all the way.

I passed through differing stages of pine, birch and juniper woodland which it was

difficult to believe had not been arranged by some landscaping genius, so beautifully composed they are. Capercaillie flitted lumpishly out of my way. Also there was a riverbed where the trees had died, presumably waterlogged. Above the tree-line I did not find the dwarf form of juniper, but that is not to say that it is not there somewhere. Isolated pines survive in the enormous open spaces of moorland. A red deer rested without cover on a steep bank, then moved away lazily, as if offended by my gaze. At several points on the moor were the old roots of pines revealed by water courses, while the ravine of a snow-fed river (with an unpronounceable name) again looked like the work of man, here as if blasted by explosives: a great sweep of rocks and gravel, brought down by flood water.

The classic walk is right round the Cairngorms from Rothiemurchus by Glen Feshie to Braemar; this is a two-day trek. An old drove road goes 37 miles from Abernethy to Braemar.

Ryvoan, *998 104*, is a naturd reserve of 300 acres, a Caledonian pine forest remnant with birch and willow. Follow the Forestry Commission track past Glenmore Lodge.

At Carrbridge, *909 223*, is the Landmark Visitors' Centre with its nature trail and sculpture park.

At Kingussie, *758 006*, pronounced Kinwissey, the folk museum is decidedly worth seeing for its wood and iron tools and utensils, and a chilling glimpse of the old Highland way of life.

Drives
For an effortless view of the Spey Valley woodlands and the surrounding mountains, drive up the ski road towards the Cairngorm. Here are two large car parks, *981 061* and *998 074*, with really wonderful views. Slightly out of season, say in June, you will have them more or less to yourself in spite of the fame and popularity of the area. You can also go by ski lift to the summit.

For a woodland drive, the B970 from Inverdruie along the east bank of the Spey to Feshiebridge picnic place is recommended. Turning off at Doune there is an Information Centre at Loch an Eilein, with a nature trail around the loch, which has a ruined castle on its island (Eileen). All is well organized and the scenery everywhere is grand and poetic.

Pine, birch, juniper and bilberry, Rothiemurchus

The view from a Cairngorm car park: Loch Morlich

SCOTLAND
Aberdeen and Speymouth

Landranger sheets 21, 27, 28, 37, 38, 45

NEAR ABERDEEN

Kirkhill Forest *853 044*, ♀ ♠, *1000 acres*, *FC*

In the pretty, hummocky countryside of Countesswells is a patchwork of small conifer woods with several easy walks. The reference given is for the most westerly. This area is very close to Aberdeen's suburbs, between the two main roads west from the city – A944, A93(T). A strip of beechwood remaining here and there adds greatly to the character of the spruce and pine. Kirkhill Forest proper, 1000 acres, is to the north and has a wayfaring course: apply to

the Forestry Commission, Aberdeen.

Within easy reach of Aberdeen (about 15 miles) is a group of large forests called, from north to south, Benachie, Banchory and Mearns, all containing Forestry Commission walks, picnic areas and special facilities for the disabled. Below we give map references for the central parking places in each, where more detailed information can be obtained. There are more than a dozen walks altogether. The Forestry Commission publishes a guidebook to its north-east Scottish forests. Names in this guidebook differ from those on the OS map.

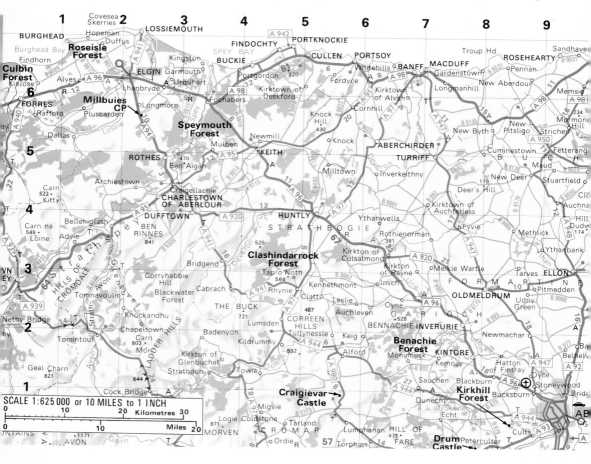

Benachie Forest: Don View Visitor Centre *672 193* and Maiden Castle *692 243*
Banchory Forest *633 944* ⎱ Section 67 map
Mearns Forest *696 801* ⎰

Drum Castle *796 005*, ♀ ♣, *411 acres, NTS*

The great square tower dates from the late thirteenth century. There is an arboretum and a woodland walk in the grounds, which are always open. The car park has a box for donations. There is supposed to be an Old Forest of Drum which is of birch, oak and Scots pines, but it has been entirely under-planted with alien shrubs. Nevertheless, it is valuable woodland with many walks and many natural history features. Information from the ranger at Crathes (Section 67).

Craigievar Castle *567 097*, ♀ ♣, *30 acres, NTS*

The pink, pepper-pot shape of the story-book castle is rather dwarfed by the regulation *Sequoiadendron* and other trees planted in the early Victorian period, and this is a shame. Such a building, surely, should dominate the scenery, which here is hilly and strongly patterned. The woodland walk is mainly through perimeter beeches and horse-chestnuts with some oaks and hollies. The parking place is beautifully organized and well kept, as are all the grounds. There is an avenue of beeches, with trunks the respectful grey of flannel.

Clashindarrock Forest ♣, *FC*

High on the moors, where there are many

Craigievar Castle was clearly designed to dominate its landscape, but it is dwarfed by North American conifers planted in the last century

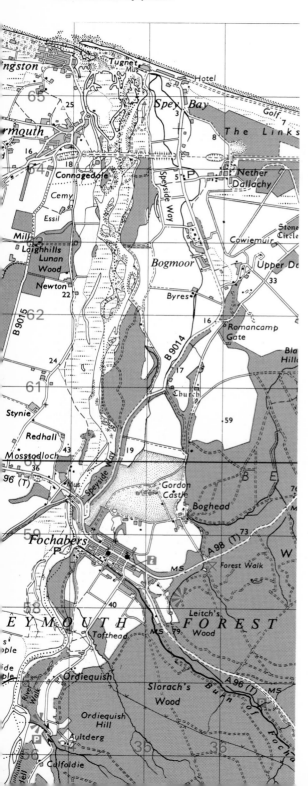

deserted farms, this vast and complex series of plantations has no formal access; but to get away from everything it is surely worth exploring. I touched only a corner at Leids Hill, *420 262*, but was impressed by the loneliness of the place and its wide skylines.

The **Forest of Deer**, on the coastal plain near Peterhead, has Forestry Commission walks and facilities at White Cow Wood, *957 514*.

Mill Cotts Estate *236 562*, ♀ ♣, *350 acres, easy fps, LA*

Amongst a string of distilleries off the A941 below Elgin, this hillside woodland and lake has three parking places and a picnic area and is generally charming and picturesque, besides being a valuable nature reserve.

Speymouth Forest *349 586*, ♣, *forest walks, FC*

The forest is enormous, but this picnic area and large car park are on a busy road. There are other points of entry. I really wanted to see the mouth of the Spey itself, that river fed by the only perpetual snows in Britain and unrivalled in its forested valley. Spey Bay is a very quiet place, and the narrow throat of the river between banks of shingle gives a refreshingly open view with clear colours. There is a walk over a disused railway viaduct at *350 642*: woodland only in respect of the low scrub of sallows and osiers – but there cannot be many viaduct walks. Up-river the mountains are a nice Scottish blue.

LAIGH OF MORAY FOREST

Near Elgin is the coastal pinewood of **Roseisle**, with the popular beach beyond and parking and picnic place in the trees at *105 655*. Popular here means that you may find a few people there on a fine day in August. Corsican pines give shelter and the sands are beautiful.

Culbin Forest *015 620 (Wellside)*, *7500 acres, 2 picnic places, FC*

To find the Wellside parking place driving west from Forres, turn right from the A96 immediately after crossing the river, and right

Roseisle, near Elgin

again at once after crossing the railway, and then right as the road suggests. Go as straight as you can for $1\frac{1}{2}$ miles (note that you are driving under wych elms at one point). Coming to a No Through Road sign, turn sharply left and then right to Wellside Farm. The parking place is beyond the farm, just inside the forest. There are two beech trees here, planted by Harold Wilson when Prime Minister and the then Secretary of State for Scotland. Wilson's tree is definitely the taller (only the native beech shows this understanding of protocol). There is another parking place at Cloddymoss, *981 600*.

The sheer mass of this forest of pines on the sands, its comparative maturity – it dates from 1921 – and its remoteness, all make it great. It is not monotonous. The dunes vary a good deal in height although most of the sands are flat, and time has allowed natural vegetation to build up. Birches, even oaks in places, and a scattering of cow wheat, suggest these were not virgin sands. A rich accretion of lichens is on every trunk and twig of the Scots pines, over

The Scots pine is the most widely distributed pine in Europe and it extends far into north Asia. Seeds from Inverness were sent to John Evelyn in Surrey in the 17th century, so it is possible that commons such as Hurt Wood have some Scottish ancestry. But continental strains are used for timber production, since remnants of the Caledonian Forest – which once covered all the Highlands up to 2000 feet – tend to derive from poorly formed trees not wanted by the timber men. However, the Scottish timber is the most durable.

Culbin Forest

moss that in summer is bright orange: the pattern is unforgettable.

Interesting though it all is, one cannot resist the pull of the shore. What happens at the edge? To find the shore from the Wellside car park, continue in the direction from which you entered for $\frac{1}{3}$ mile, then follow the forest road as it turns left. After about $\frac{1}{3}$ mile (passing a group of lodgepole pines on your right) turn

right. You are now heading for the shore, and following the ride, which becomes a footpath, you climb a rise of nearly 100 feet to a triangulation point. Here you can see the shore. It is not, usually, sea, but an expanse of wet sand.

Here I waited while a great sky, a mess of clouds like a celestial scene painter's accident, failed to clear enough for the photographs I

wanted. The mountains of Easter Ross glowed
with fairy light, the Moray Firth gleamed, but
the great amphitheatre of the shore, where I
was the only spectator, remained in grey dusk
except for an occasional dim gleam of reflected
light. As I waited, feeling small in this great
solitude, I watched the daylight fade. The
present enlarged and my schedule diminished.
The sand gleamed with millions of worm casts;
even the pine forest seemed insignificant.

What happens where the trees stop? Grasses
begin, patterned with rings of sea asters.

The Darnaway Forest, to the south, is
private, but has waymarked paths and a
Visitors' Centre at Tearie Farm, *989 569*.

Sea aster, Culbin Sound

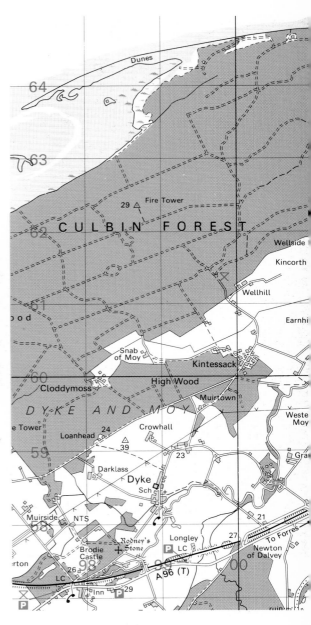

There are, of course, woods on the western side of the region and by the coastal lochs are three important nature reserves. Inverpolly (NNR, 42 square miles) adjoins Ben Mor Coigach, *080 070* (RSNC and SWT, 22 square miles). These are at 'the heart of one of the two 200 square miles of Britain . . . where no man sleeps', wrote James Fisher in 1966. There are relict woodlands around and on the islands of the lochs. A smaller reserve is Inchnadamph, *250 215* (NNR, 3200 acres). 'A limestone oasis with complex geology, rare flowers and willows', wrote Fisher.

Passing through the Kyle of Sutherland into the Shin Forest you enter a semi-Arctic region where birch is the dominant native tree. The luxuriant vegetation of the Achany Glen and Strath Oykel disappears, and the low hills are bare except for frequent stretches of Forestry Commission afforestation, cast around like clothes of green, and looking warm. Great clammy buttocks of mountains rise above lochs where a scattering of birches and one or two alders are the usual complement of trees. The birches climb the steep lochsides and cling in the burn sides, hardly ever forming woodlands.

It was not always so. Large pines are preserved as black logs in the peat. The most northerly group of native pine now surviving is at Glen Einig.

A little further south in the Amat Forest near Croick, the surveyor Robertson in the eighteenth century wrote of pines with 30- or 40-foot-long uninterrupted trunks, $8\frac{1}{2}$ feet in circumference: a stump of a tree 3 feet 9 inches in diameter.

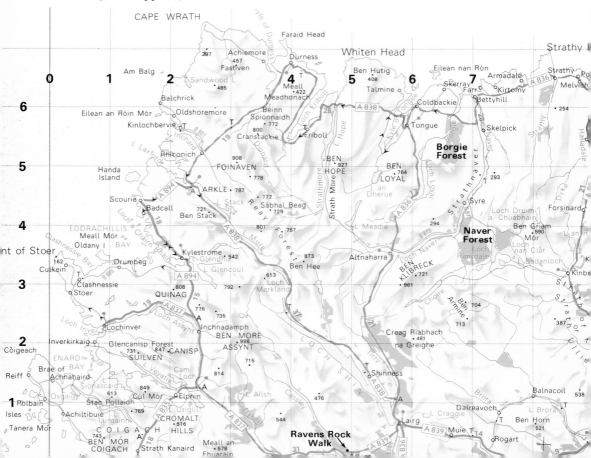

SHIN FOREST

The Drumliah Walk *603 929, 1¾m*
This walk begins from a lay-by in larchwoods
1 mile north of Bonar Bridge on the A836.

The Shin Falls Walk *576 993, 1½m*
The walk is on each side of the river. There are
good facilities, with a café 'open seven days a
week' with loud music and moderately priced
salmon sandwiches. Signposted from the A836,
the road, B864, is actually parallel on the
opposite side of the glen.

Carbisdale Castle Walk *575 955, 2¼m*
Turn off the A9 at Ardgay on to the Culrain
road – before Bonar Bridge. The walk starts
in the castle grounds, through varied woodland
to a small loch.

Ravens Rock Walk *500 010, 1½m, riverside*
Nowhere in particular, the cark park, very
pleasant amongst pines, is very easy to find
from the Rosehall to Lairg road or the Rosehall
to Bonar Bridge road. The walk is a set piece
and quite splendid: larches are poised on
precipices over the narrow gorge of a small
river, where everything green has its own way.
Piles of dead branches are covered in green
moss, ferns compete for space among lichens,
and large North American trees add grandeur
to the wild scenery. Douglas firs with perfect
stems are in the majority, but there are fine
spruces and a Nikko fir. There are beeches too:
beeches here have trunks streaked in two tones
of grey with patches of dark moss.

There are fine groves of alder and good-
looking oaks among the birches of Strath
Oykel: forestry in Glen Oykel.

Naver Forest, Syre *691 428*, ✚ ☙ *(ruins),*
1½m, FC
The car park is reached by a stretch of forest
road from the tiny village of Syre. The woods

Rich vegetation from a Ravens Rock viewpoint

SCALE 1:625 000 or 10 MILES to 1 INCH
0   10   20 Kilometres 30
0   10   Miles 20

of spruce and pine are planted around the site of a deserted village which has been thoroughly researched and provided with well-written and illustrated information panels set in stone cairns. The site is described as a bright green island among the moors. One query raised by the thoughtful writers of the text is about the high fertility (still) of the soil. Did the villagers apply phosphates? they ask. Well, in a way I suppose they must have done. Why did they not expand their very limited crop-growing land? I think that the answer to the second question is that they were too tired, after wresting all their needs from this wind-swept

Flowers of the field, Shin Forest

(and snowed-on) hillside, and probably severely undernourished, if the diet described here is correct (porridge and more porridge). The poor people kept beef cattle, but rarely ate meat, the beef being taken on the hoof to the markets in the south. They used everything they could lay hands on to manure 'lazy beds'

still visible by the various coloured grasses on the site: they had no woodland, at least not close at hand: the peat provided hard timber (bog pine, rare enough to be handed down for generations), fuel, building blocks, and roofing and insulation. Stones, still in position on the site, indicate the base walls of the houses. Simple furniture was of birch, probably, utensils of oak.

The cattle were kept in the houses in winter, and in times of famine were bled, the blood added to the gruel. In the summer the cattle ate the moor grass. Sheep were delicate, with fine wool, and were put to bed at night.

A more hardy breed of sheep that would stay on the moors all year was developed in the early nineteenth century. The value of the land rose from tuppence per acre with people and cattle to two shillings per acre with sheep and no people. So the people were evicted by their landlords, who by this time were either English or, if Scots, had got English habits. If the

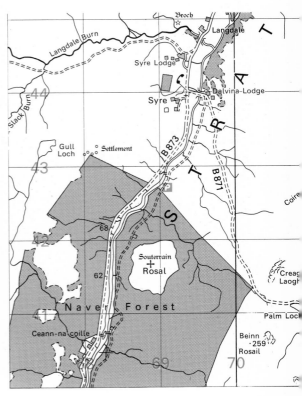

people would not go their houses were
destroyed and the roof trees burnt, these last
being apparently the property of the landlord.
The people were given their own crofts on the
coast and had to learn to fish the sea. At Rosal
there is no evidence of burning and it is
assumed that the villagers left when they were
told to – perhaps they were glad to go, or had
left some time before. All this is explained in
much more detail on the site. It is a moving
experience and the Forestry Commission is to
be complimented on the way it has handled the
whole thing, even if you can 'take it with a
pinch of salt'.

The village is marked on the map as Rosal:
Souterrain. This applies to a long chambered
tomb in the centre of the village dating from
the Stone Age. There are also some Stone Age
huts; it is believed that human occupation was
continuous up to the coming of the mountain
sheep. It is extraordinary that the prehistoric
tombs and dwellings should have remained in
the centre of the village. Perhaps the ancestry
was direct, forefathers always respected.

The soil is fertile. And yet, for all those
centuries the community remained small.
What an extraordinary balance was preserved
between the size of the village and the harsh
environment! In mediaeval England,
unwanted babies were left out to die – perhaps
the same method was used here to keep the
population down to the size the land could
support. Even so the question 'why didn't they
enlarge the fertile fields?' remains an
interesting one and the limiting factor is not
properly known. The pattern, in the
Highlands, is always of emigration. Young men
and girls, perhaps, went south with the cattle
and did not return.

Borgie Forest 665 586, ♠, 4000 acres, 2 short walks, FC

As you approach the shore of the Stormy Sea,
the knuckles of rock begin to show through the
thin flesh of peat and there are frequent
lochans above sea-level. The great forest
around the River Borgie is not quite the most
northerly one; that of Strathy to the east is
slightly further out. There are firs here that
predate the Forestry Commission, at least one

being a really beautiful *Abies procera* var.
glauca – and more have been planted near the
forest road; spruce is within. The shortest
walks are not a way of seeing the forest: I drove
for a mile or so but there was little more to see.
From the hills above one gets an impression of
some variety in the forest, but from within
little appears except acres of spruce. I am not
complaining; the coastal views are stunning.

A large, sandy beach – in Tongue Bay
(Gaelic *Tunga*) with a good view of the Rabbit
Islands – was deserted except for two people at
4.00 pm on a fine Sunday in August. High
above Tongue I watched a strangely shaped
half mile of sand being gently licked away by
the waves of that cold sea.

Leaves of *Abies procera*, Borgie Forest

Stones of the lonely deserted village of Rosal

Borgie Forest and Ben Loyal

Index